FRANCESCO FEDERICO MANCINI
GIOVANNA CASAGRANDE

W9-BGD-889

PERUGIA
HISTORICAL AND ARTISTIC GUIDE

éditions
ITALCARDS
Modena italy

Holder of sole rights of sale:
PELLEGRINI - 06100 Perugia - Via Cialdini, 16
Tel. 43.766 - 500.82.53

PRESENTATION

Perugia is situated at 493 meters above sea level, on top of some hills sloping gently down towards the Tiber valley. From its high terraces it is possible to enjoy a vast panorama, with Monte Tezio and the mountains of Gubbio towards the north, Monte Subasio and the Appenines towards the east, Monte Malbe towards the west and the broad expanse of Tuscany and Latium towards the south.

Up until the nineteen-fifties, the image of Perugia appeared very similar to the one described by travelers and artists from previous epochs: viewed from a distance, the city displayed a compact profile enclosed by the city walls and framed by the vegetation growing on the hillside. The choices of modern urbanization have profoundly modified this image and caused the city to lose much of its original physiognomy. It was above all during the building «boom» of the Sixties that Perugia acquired its present aspect, as it expanded and formed new city suburbs, mainly in a convulsive and irrational manner. Today the population comprises more than 130,000 inhabitants distributed over a very extensive area. The city is the seat of local government for both the province and the region. A busy centre of agriculture, industry and commerce, Perugia is also a prestigious tourist destination.

For centuries, Perugia's location along the main axis linking the Adriatic and Tyrrhenian seas has secured for the city a considerable strategic and economic importance. It is no coincidence that old sources place Perugia on the same level as Siena and Florence («the three Communes»). The power and wealth of the city are reflected in its monuments, a tangible sign of a past rich in history.

The layout of the ancient city is characterized by a nucleus of Etruscan origins, enclosed by walls in travertine, which are in their turn surrounded by a fortified wall built during the Medieval era (14th cent.) in order to protect the five boroughs edified upon the ridges extending from the hilltop. This extension gave the city a star-like configuration that Leon Battista Alberti (15th cent.) efficaciously compared to the fingers of a hand.

The numerous landmarks to be found in the city centre arise from a dense urban tissue characterized by silent, suggestive squares, narrow, tortuous streets and flights of steps that wind their way up and down amidst the walls of houses, linking the various levels of the city.

Immersed in these splendid memories, Perugia lives with the pace of modern society and yet preserves an atmosphere of peaceful tranquillity. The presence of two universities, one for foreign students and the other for Italians, confers a vital, culturally dynamic role upon the city.

A variety of important musical and theatrical events are also held there.

Historical background

Perugia is a typical example of an Etruscan and Roman city. For centuries its urban area was confined within the powerful city walls of the *urbs vetus*. After the year 1000, it began to expand progressively until the thirteenth century and first half of the fourteenth century, when the outlying hamlets became an integrated part of the city surrounded by a new city wall.

Like all Etruscan strongholds, Perugia is located on a hill (493 metres above sea level). It is not known for sure when the original urban nucleus was formed (6th century B.C.?). Traditionally, Perugia was the seat of one of the 12 «lucomonie», a clear indication of its importance as an Etruscan town. The ancient walls (6th-2nd century B.C.) and its various hypogeums are also evidence of this fact.

After the year 1200, Perugia became part of the Roman domain. Its fidelity to Rome continued even after the defeat of the Romans at Trasimeno (217 B.C.) during the Punic War. After 90 B.C., Perugia was conceded Roman city status.

There is no documentation of the important events in which the town participated up to the *Bellum Perusinum* when it became the centre of the quarrel between Octavian and Lucian Antony, brothers of Mark Antony. Besieged, the city surrendered in 40 B.C., was burnt and partially destroyed. Following this event, Octavian Augustus had the town rebuilt and it became part of the 7th Administrative Region (*Augusta Perusia*). Shortly after the middle of the 3rd century A.D., the Perugian Emperor, Vibio Treboniano Gallo awarded the city the title of «ius coloniae» (*Colonia Vibia*).

The exact period in which Christianity was spread to Perugia is unknown although, presumably, this occurred from the very first centuries onwards; by the mid-5th century, the Perugian Diocese had already been formed. In the political void of this period, the Bishop represented the only form of religious and civil authority; indicative of this fact is the episode involving Bishop Herculanus who, as leader of the Perugian resistance during the siege by the Gothic King Totila, was martyred by him after the defeat of the city. With the end of the Greek/Gothic war (535-553), Perugia returned into Byzantine hands, becoming part of the strip of territorial land connecting Rome to Ravenna (the Byzantine Corridor), and a seat of the Exarchate.

The centuries leading up to the year 1000 are in the darkest in the history of Perugia. Althouth threatened and sometimes occupied, Perugia never fell to the political reign of the Longobardi who had conquered the nearby Dukedom of Spoleto; if anything,it was one of the cities under papal government. The advent of the year 1000 brought with it signs of social and political activity; as well as the Bishop, there were judges and «boni homines».

We do not know about the early phases of the Perugian commune which, by 1139, had already been in existence for sometime. In fact, during this same year, the inhabitants of the Polvese Isle and Lake Trasimeno made an act of submission to the *civitas Perusina*, represented on the occasion by ten Consuls, the largest number possessed by any town at this time. During the second half of the 7th century, Perugia extended its dominion in various directions to include Gubbio, Città di Castello, Città della Pieve and towards the Trasimeno and Chiano Vallies. In 1184, it conquered Castiglione del Lago and began its conquest of the particularly fertile Chiugi area. In 1186, Emperor Henry VI conceded to Perugia the government of its «contado» by way of recognition of an already irrefutable fact. In 1198, Pope Innocence III took the city under his protection.

Being free of the Imperial Yoke, protected and favoured by the papal authorities and consistently Guelf (Ghibelline unrest was quashed as in the era of Corradino di Svevia), in the 13th century, Perugia was able to assert itself as a strong and powerful commune. It continued its policy of expansion conquering Assisi, Nocera, Gualdo, Montone and Cagli and was engaged in bitter fighting with Foligno. It had a city population of about 28,000 with 45,000 in the «contado»; alongside the original feudal nobility, a new bourgeoisie of merchants, artisans and lawyers etc. developed: in 1286, the varions artisan guilds numbered 41; the Mint and the University were instituted;

public works, such as the aqueduct and the Great Fountain, were carried out; statutory laws were elaborated — the oldest statute of the city is dated 1279. Charitable institutions established themselves in the expanding quarters of the city in which several Popes chose to reside; indeed, four Conclaves were held there (1216, 1265, 1285 and 1294); many fairs were held such as the All Saints' Fair documented as early as 1260; the Discipline movement fostered by Raniero Fasani spread from Perugia (1250) throughout Europe; the city possessed two guest magistrates: the Captain of the People and the Podestà. The city was divided into five rioni (quarters) according to its porte (city gates) (porta Sole, porta St.

Pietro, porta Eburnea, porta St. Susanna, porta St. Angelo).

During the first half of the 12th century, the first decades of Pope Avignone's reign, Perugia became even more independent in the assertion of its predominance. From 1303, the city's government was in the hands of Priors elected by the Guilds (numbering 10-2 for each porta): this was the heyday of the guild-based commune. The important vulgate constitution dated 1342.

The black plague of 1348 also claimed victims from Perugia. The city gave further proof of its strength when, in 1358,it fought against the Cortonese and Sienese peoples (the Victory of Torrita).

The internal quarrels between the «nobles» (beccherini) and the «popular class» (raspanti), the attempts of the Papacy from 1350 onwards to subject the cities of Umbria to its authority, the war with Pope Urban V, ending with the Peace Treaty of Bologna (1370) in which Perugia recognised its subordinacy to the Ro-

1. Perugia, seen from St. Peter's Gate. 2. View.

5

man Church and the Pope, all signalled the beginning of the city's political decline.

From 1370 onwards, Perugia was placed under the control of papal delegates; one of these, Gerard du Puy, Abbot of Monmaggiore, in order to keep a tighter hold on the city, had a fortress built at the porta Sole, linking it with the other one in the quarter of St. Antony. In 1375, the Perugians revolted and forced the detested Abbot out of the city, destroying both fortresses. Notwithstanding the banishment of the papal delegate, Perugia continued to be divided by internal party quarrels throughout the last 20 years of the 14th century.

At the beginning of the 15th century, the popular party, who had been led by Biordo Michelotti, killed in 1398, was in power, threatened, however, by the nobles. The popular government had to seek external support - first, from Gian Galeazzo Visconti, Governor of Milan (1400), then from the Church (1403) and then from Ladislao di Durazzo (1408). The power of the popular party declined between 1416 and 1424 and the governorship of Perugia was taken over by the famous mercenary captain, Braccio Fortebracci da Montone. After this, the city turned once more to the Church. The governorship of Nicolò Piccinino, another mercenary, proved to be little more than a shadow of the preceding one.

The political government of «democratic» Perugia became more and more oligarchical and feudal, progressively losing all forms of political initiative.

Among the families of the «old» and «new» nobility who were destined to from the oligarchical clique which would pull the strings of government in Perugia and the surroundig area are the following names: Baglioni, Oddi, Montesperelli, Montemelini, Arcipreti, Cavaceppi and Alfani — all descended from Bartolo da Sassoferrato — Paolucci, Tassi, Randoli, Corgna, dell'Antognolla, della Penna, Cinaglia, Graziani, Bontempi, Ranieri, Sciri, Mansueti, Armanni, Coromani and Signorelli etc. An important member of the Baglioni family was Braccio (died 1479), the so-called Lorenzo the Magnificent of Perugia; he too was a mercenary by profession. In 1471, he took part in the institution of Perugia's first printing guild.

During the 15th century, the eco-

nomic strength of the «bourgeois» nobility and the «feudalised bourgeoisie» was based on territorial possession as well as on the predominance of certain key sectors of commerce and production.

15th-century Perugia — disturbed by feuds between the families of the oligarchy (Baglioni, Oddi, etc.) and by continual party struggles — was living a double reality: on the one hand, corruption and moral decadence and, on the other, religious fervour and moralistic ideals spread by the great Franciscan preachers such as Bernardino da Siena and Bernardino da Feltre. In 1462, Perugia's first pawnbrokers institution was established.

After betrayals and blood-shed in which members of the Baglioni family turned against and killed eachother (the «Bloody Wedding» of 1500), Giampaolo I and Malatesta IV, both of the said family and both mercenaries, «governed» Perugia during the first decade of the 16th century.

One was beheaded by Pope Leone X in 1520. The other defended the Florentine Republic against Pope Clement VII's army in 1529 (not without accusations of betrayal). However, not even the Baglioni succeded in establishing a governorship similar to that of the Medici family in Florence mainly because of the city's close proximity to Rome; indeed, the city was heading towards the total and definitive loss of its independence.

During the 17th century and most of the 18th century, Perugia was not the scene of great events. A certain «disorder» brought about the Castro War (1641-1644) between Urban VIII and his feudal lord, Odoardo Farnese.

Throughout the 17th century, the city's economic wealth was based on the agricultural nobility who had undertaken public offices. Associations, such as the Merchant's Guild and the Exchange, had undergone a complete transformation: from free associations for members of the relative trades, they had become exclusive institutions for the nobility.

The long period of «order» was shattered by the French invasion in which Perugia became part of the Trasimeno department with a consequent revival of the middle classes.

1. The Medieval walls of Porta St. Anthony. 2. The area around Porta St. Angelo.

7

The Main Square

(Piazza 4 Novembre)

The commune's main square — *platea comunis* or *platea magna* — was the centre of civil and religious power. In this area, the most ancient public building on record was the Consul's Place, later the Podestà's Palace, which was located in the area around the Maestà delle Volte Church. Several fires and the reconstruction works carried out during the second half of the 16th century left no trace of this palace. The arches visible on the façade of the existing Bishop's Palace are perhaps remnants of the building's reconstruction carried out around 1422-1423. The building in question was linked to the St. Lawrence presbytery to the north and to the Bishop's Palace to the south; the latter is thought to have been placed further back than the existing one.

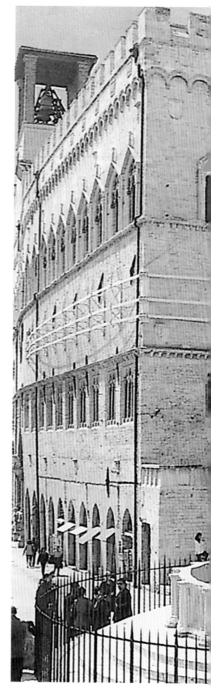

The Main Square: the Great Fountain and the Priors' Palace.

The Prior's Palace

(Palazzo dei Priori)

A new residential palace for the highest ranking political authority of the city-state was thought of as early as 1270; by 1298, an early nucleus of the palace is thought to have already existed, comprising the work of two local master-builders: Giacomo di Servadio and Giovannello di Benvenuto. From 1300 onwards, the Commune succeeded in making the necesssary expropriations for the definitive construction of the *palatium novum comunis Perusii*. Amongst the buildings demolished to make way for the enlarged palace was the parish Church of St. Severo di Piazza. The construction work went on until 1353. From 1429 to 1443, a further extension was carried out.

The later structural additions on the South side date from the late 16th century (1576-1588).

The palace is built in local Travertine and white and red Bettona rock and presents a compact and wall-like solidity. It is, however, animated by expressive decorative motifs and by the asymmetrical arrangement of spaces as on the side facing the fountain: here, the main portal is offcentre with respect to the façade and the levels of the two ensembles left and right of the fan-shaped staircase are different from eachother. This does not mean that the palace is lacking in stylistic unity or architectural coherence. These are guaranteed by the closely-placed succession of elegant mullioned and lancet windows placed in a rectangular display (lower level) and surmounted by a triangular apex (upper level). The

1

façade which looks onto the fountain has a wide, semi-circular staircase, built in 1902, the old version (designed by Ambrogio Maitani) having been destroyed at the end of the 16th century. From the first landing on the right, a staircase leads to the Vaccari Sala, the ancient seat of the Communal Cadastre (the iron door bears the initials «A.G.» — *Armarium Generale* — and the inscription:

«*MCCCXXXVIII Giulius Rufinelli me fecit*»). Above the great ogival door there are two travertine corbels which acted as supports for the splendid mediaeval bronzes (late 13th-century) of the Griffin, emblem of the city, and the Lion, which are now preserved in a hall within the Palace. The same door leads to the Notaries' room, originally an assembly hall for the people of Perugia. This is a majestic rectangular hall whose vault is supported by eight powerful Romanic arches.

Returning to the exterior, before proceeding along the side of the building, there is a 14th-century portico with irregular arches on Roman-style capitals, two of which were made by «Vester Lutii»; this indicates the former site of the Church of St. Severo which was demolished at the beginning of the 13th century to make way for the extension of the palace. The façade overlooking the Corso follows a curved line — obviously to adapt the extension to fit in with the

1. The Priors' Palace. 2. The IV November's Square.

preexisting houses further back. Besides a progression of mullioned and lancet windows which lighten the solid horizontal effect of the wall, there is an elaborate rounded doorway attributed to various artists from Perugia, Siena, Florence and the North of Italy. On each side of the door there are pillars supported by lions: the one on the right bears allergorical sculptures of Generosity, Fertility and Pride; the one on the left shows Avarice, Greed and Humility. The pillars are surmounted by two griffins subjugating calves, symbols of the Butcher Trade which provided the majority of the funds for the realization of the project. In the splay of the portal, placed whithin animalistic and plant-like decorative motifs, the are 58 allegorical motifs which are often difficult to interpret. Finally, there are three statues of St. Louis of Toulouse, St. Lawrence and St. Herculanus.

Within the palace, on the third floor, there are the headquarters of the Communal Administration. Of note, is the fine Gothic structure of the atrium with crossvaulting supported by powerful columns. This floor is host to murals by Giovanni Schepers and Dono Doni (Sala Rossa), Giovan Battista Lombardelli (Urban Office), Bernardino Pinturicchio (Sala Consiliare), and Paolo Brizi (the Mayor's Apartment). The decoration (much repainted) of the vault and walls of the Sala Gialla, formerly the Chapel of the Priors' Palace, are probably the work of Matteuccio Salvucci.

1. The Priors' Palace: the door facing onto Corso Vannucci. 2. The Priors' Palace: the Notaries' Room.

12

The National Gallery of Umbria

The Gallery is on the third floor. It is the most important collection of mediaeval and modern art in the whole region. Its origins are in the state confiscations of the first French Republic and the Napoleonic Empire in which many works of the city's churches, convents and monasteries were gathered together under one roof: the Monastery of Monte Morcino Nuovo, especially provided by the Napoleonic régime. This concession was confirmed by Pope Pius VII during the Restoration. In 1861, in accordance with the Pepoli decree, designed to suppress religious associations, numerous other works were added to the Gallery which, in 1863, was named after Pietro Vannucci, alias the "Perugino". In 1879, all the material was transferred to the top floor of the Priors' Palace. In 1907, on occasion of the famous exhibition of Umbrian Sacred Art, this rich and well documented collection, arranged by Francesco Moretti, was officially inaugurated. During the period 1952-55, further ac-

quisitions and, above all, the prevalence of new ideas regarding exposition techniques, led to a new arrangement of the material by Gisberto Martelli and Francesco Santi. The recent acquisition of greater exhibition space, including the large Podiani Hall, formerly the «Augusta» Communal Library, has brought about a further extension of the Gallery which now includes work from the Italian Cinquecento to Settecento.

Medieval section (12th-14th cent.): frescoes removed from the walls of churches and convents, mainly Perugian; wooden crucifix from the Roman epoch taken from the church of S.Maria di Roncione near Deruta; head of Christ, again carved out of wood, from Montone; large painted cross from the church of S.Francesco al Prato, dated 1272 and attributed to an artist, probably Umbrian, commonly known as the «Maestro di S. Francesco»; some sections of an altar front by the same painter and to which might also belong the two-faced processional cross n. 18; altar front by a Giottesque artist, known as the «Maestro del Farneto» after the place where the work

was found; altar front by Giano dell'Umbria displaying a refined Byzantinesque language, inspired by Roman models; small tabernacle with accents of intense expressive drama and characteristics strongly influenced by popular styles; polyptych by Vigoroso da Siena, a follower of Cimabue (ca. 1290); Madonna and Child by Duccio di Boninsega from Siena; two sculpted panels belonging to the Fontana Maggiore of Perugia (she-wolf breast-feeding the twins and Rome), the first one attributed to Nicola Pisano and the second to Giovanni; sculptures by Arnolfo di Cambio taken from the dismantled fountain «in pede plateae» (1281); polychrome wood sculpture from the first quarter of the 14th cent., taken from the church of S.Agostino; numerous works by the Sienese artist Meo, who was ac-

tive in Perugia between about 1320 and 1330; altarpiece taken from the Badia Celestina, signed by Marino da Perugia, an artist trained in the Giotto style who was open to Sienese and Riminese cultural influences; works by 14th century Perugian artists displaying a fresh narrative style (Mastro del Dossale di Paciano, Maestro dei dossali di Subiaco, Maestro della Maestà delle Volte).

The Medieval goldwork is also of great interest. Worthy of note are: the chalice and paten of Benedict

1. The «Maestro di St. Francesco»: Crucifixion (13th century). 2. Duccio di Boninsegna: Madonna and Child (14th century). 3. Arnolfo di Cambio: A Scribe (13th century).

ni brothers, altarpiece by Lello da Velletri, polyptych by Bicci di Lorenzo, Madonna and Child with Saints by Ottaviano Nelli, Madonna and Child by Gentile da Fabriano).

Early Renaissance section (15th cent.): polyptych by Beato Angelico (ca. 1445) completed for the Guidalotti chapel in S.Domenico; polyptych by Piero della Francesca taken from the monastery of S.Antonio da Padova in Perugia (ca. 1470); Madonna and Child with Saints signed and dated (1456) by Benozzo Gozzoli; fresco by Domenico Veneziano, a highly damaged fragment from the imposing gallery of illustrious men completed around 1438 in the later destroyed Palazzo di Braccio Baglioni; bronze low-relief portraying the Flagellation by the Sienese artist Giovanni Boccati, a refined, lyrical interpreter of Lippi, Angelico and

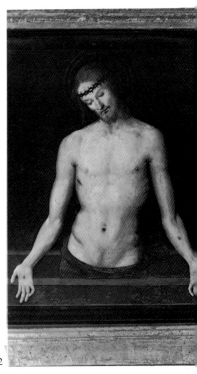

XI, refined works from the early 14th century; paten with Annunciation by Ugolino di Vieri; reliquary of S.Giuliana; chalice and paten signed by Cataluccio da Todi and which may be dated to about 1380. There are also some precious ivories, including the top of a Romanesque pastoral staff (late 12th cent.), a statuette with the Madonna and Child, almost certainly French (late 13th cent.), two caskets from the workshop of the Embriaghis.

Late Gothic section (end of the 14th cent. to the middle of the 15th cent.): works by Sienese artists (Luca di Tommè, Bartolo di Fredi, Taddeo di Bartolo, Lippo Vanni, Niccol di Buonaccorso, Jacopo di Mino del Pelliciaio); works by artists from Florence, Umbria and the Marches (fresco by the Salimbe-

Domenico Veneziano; paintings by Matteo da Gualdo, Niccolò di Liberatore - known as the «l'Alunno» (the pupil) - the Perugian artists Benedetto Bonfigli, Bartolomeo Caporali and Fiorenzo di Lorenzo; fragmentary sculptures by Agostino di Duccio (ca. 1475) taken from the church of the Maest delle Volte. The display includes a visit to the Cappella dei Priori, decorated by Benedetto Bonfigli (ca. 1455-1480) and featuring stories from the lives of the saints Ludovico and Ercolano (the work,

1. Benedetto Bonfigli (?): the Assault of the Captain (15th century). 2. Pietro Perugino: Christ in the Tomb (16th century). 3. Fiorenzo di Lorenzo: the Adoration of the Shepherds (15th century). 4. Gentile da Fabriano: Madonna and Child (15th century).

4

17

partially completed in 1461, was inspected by Fra Filippo Lippi).

Section dedicated to Perugino and his followers: Adoration of the Magi, attributed to Perugino by Vasari and today considered one of his first works; eight small paintings portraying the miracles of S.Bernandino (1473) and placed around a gonfalon by Benedetto Bonfigli (different masters were involved in the execution of these works, including Perugino and Pintoricchio); the Dead Christ and Madonna dei Battuti, both by Perugino (ca. 1495); sections of the large ancona of S.Agostino completed by Perugino between 1507 and 1523; altarpiece of S.Maria dei Fossi by Pintoricchio (1495); numerous paintings by artists active

in the first half of the sixteenth century, mostly Umbrians, who developed the style of Perugino and were eventually to unite and combine it with the nascent phenomenon after the styles of Raphael and Michelangelo, thus representing a cultural bridge between the classicism of the early sixteenth century and the experiences of mannerism (Giannicola di Paolo, Giovan Battista Caporali, Berto di Giovanni, Domenico Alfani, Pompeo Cocchi, Dono Doni, Orazio Alfani).

Late Mannerism section, seventeenth and eighteenth centuries: large altarpiece by Cristoforo Gherardi, known as the «Doceno» and Lattanzio Pagani (1549), taken from the church of S.Maria del Popolo; Adoration of the Shepherds by Arrigo Fiammingo (1563); works by artists adopting a Baroque style (Francesco Barocci, Vincenzo Pellegrini, known as the «Pittor Bello», Simeone Ciburri, Benedetto Bandiera); Presentation at the Temple by Andrea Sacchi, taken from the church of S.Filippo Neri; Nativity of Mary by Pietro

1. Bernardino Pinturicchio: Madonna and Child with St. John (16th century). 2. Giovan Battista Caporali: Madonna and Child (16th century). 3. Piero della Francesca: the Annunciation (15th century).

3

da Cortona, also taken from S.Filippo Neri; Mystic Nuptials of Saint Catherine, by Pietro da Cortona, on loan from the Fine Arts Academy; Saint Cecily and the Angel by Orazio Gentileschi; works by Umbrian artists (Giovanni Antonio Scaramuccia, Luigi Scaramuccia, Giovanni Domenico Cerrini and G.B.Pacetti, known as «lo Sguazzino»); painting by Corrado Giaquinto; sketch by Francesco Trevisani; paintings by Sebastiano Conca; large painting by Ludovico Mazzanti; altarpiece by Pierre Subleyras from the church of Montemorcino Nuovo; paintings by Francesco Mancini (1732), Giuseppe Maria Crespi, Giovanni Odazzi, Giacinto Boccanera, Anton Maria Fabrizi, Francesco Busti.

1. Domenico Alfani: Madonna and Child between SS. George and Nicholas of Bari (16th century). 2. Agostino di Duccio: Madonna with Child (15th century). 3. Giovanni Antonio Scaramuccia: Madonna with Child between SS. Dominic and Catherine of Siena (17th century).

The Cathedral of St. Lawrence

(Duomo)

The Cathedral of Perugia originally stood in the area in which the
Abbey of St. Peter is now located;
it was then transferred to the area
around St. Stephen's of Castellare,
near the ancient city wall. Around
the year 1000, the Cathedral was
moved again to the city centre. In
1036, a refectory, other than the
one reserved for the bishops, was
certainly in existence. This proves
that the Cathedral Church already
had its own clerical community.

It was during the 16th century
that the church took on its present-
day appearance. Before that, it had
been disposed and arranged in a
different way. The original order
for the construction of a cathedral
church dates back to the year 1300;
the works were entrusted to the supervision of Fra Bevignate, a Sives-
trine monk. Notwithstanding this,
its present form was acquired during the 15th century. As well as
bearing the titular dedication to St.
Lawrence, it was also given the title of St. Herculanus — the *defensor civitatis* bishop who was martyred by the Gothic King Totila according to a story by Gregorio
Magno. During the «communal»
epoch, Bishop Herculanus was the
city's figure-head. Up to the 17th
century, his remains were preserved
in a specially-built chapel within the
Cathedral walls; the walls of this
chapel are still visible behind the
statue of Julius III.

On the side facing the piazza, the
arches of the **Loggia di Braccio** lean
against the walls. The loggia dates
from 1423 and is a monument of
early-Renaissance architecture, attributed to Fioravante Fioravanti
from Bologna. Below the Loggia, a
section of Roman wall is visible. We
can also see part of the base of the
cathedral's former bell-tower as well

as a copy of the Rock of Justice
which is now preserved in the Pri-
or's Palace. This is an object of considerable interest. Dating from
1234, it was constructed by the commune in order to mark the payment
of alla public debts and to establish
the payment of taxes according to
a census (*per libram*).

On this side of the church, the
bronze statue of Julius III, placed
on a high pedestal, was made by the
young Vincenzo Danti in 1555 to
celebrate the Pope's restitution of
the city's principal magistrates. The
large, solid door is the work of L.

The Cathedral of St. Lawrence.

22

Scalza (1568), based on drawings by Galeazzo Alessi. A niche above the tympanum of the door contains a wooden crucifix by Polidoro Ciburri, placed here by the people of Perugia in 1540 during the 'salt war', as an act of defiance against the Pope. The elegant Renaissance pulpit, right of the door, was erected during the first decade of the 15th century and it was from here that Bernardino of Siena preached in 1425 and 1427. Not far off, on a protruding column, there are two vertically placed niches; the higher one held a bronze statue by the Donatellian sculpture, Bellano da Padova. It represented Pope Paul II and was melted down by the French in 1798.

The principal façade, overlooking piazza Danti, has an impressive 18th-century doorway, built by Pietro Carattoli by order of Bishop Antonio Ansidei. The bell-tower was built between 1606 and 1612 by Valentino Martelli and was probably based on a design by Bino Sozi.

Inside the church, right of the door, the tomb of Bishop G.A. Baglioni back onto the inner-façade wall. This is attributed to Urbano da Cortona. On the left, is the sepulchral monument of Bishop Marcantonio Oddi by Domenico Guidi, a pupil of Algardi. Above, within a frame of elaborate gold-plated stucco, is the great altar-piece by Giovanni Antonio Scaramuccia (1610-1611), original-

ly destined for the Chapel of the Commune of Perugia in the church of St. Mary of the Angels. At the beginning of the north aisle is the Chapel of the Holy Ring which contains the venerated relic of the Virgin's wedding ring, taken from Chiusi in 1473. The chapel was once decorated with frescoes by Pinturicchio. Now, a painting by G.B. Wicar is placed above the altar, substituting a painting of the same subject by Pietro Perugino, at present in the Museum of Caen. The altar is host to the precious reliquary of the Holy Ring by Bino di Pietro and Federico and Cesanno del Roscetto, a masterpiece of Italian Renaissance gold-smith work. Immediately following the side-door, we come across an altar of the Banner with a painting at-

tributed to Berto di Giovanni (1526) and a lunette by Giannicola di Paolo. Further on, attached to the walls, are fragments of the Pietà altar, built by Agostino di Duccio around 1473 and demolished in 1625. The northern wing of the transept forms the Crucifix Chapel, the altar of which (the work of Pietro Carattoli), bears a carved wooden Crucifix dating from the 15th century. The chapel on the left-hand side of the apse contains a large canvas by Ippolito Borghesi (1624) depicting the Assumption of the Virgin Mary and frescoes by Francesco Appiani. The hectagonal apse, besides accomodating a splendid wooden choir by Giuliano da Maiano and Domenico del Tasso (1491), is host to two oil paintings by Baldassarre Orsini (1767) and two by Carlo Spiridione Mariotti (1768). The altar of the next chapel, named after St. Emidio, is decorated by a canvas by Francesco Appiani (1784). The south wing of the transept contains the Chapel of St. Stephen. This was once completely covered with frescoes by Giovanni Baglione (1609 circa). Two small side-doors lead into the Oratory of St. Onofrio, built in 1484, in order to accomodate the altar-piece by Luca Signorelli which is today preserved in the Cathedral Museum. The frescoes on the ceiling are by Domenico Bruschi (1877). Further along the south aisle is the Chapel of the Sacrament, built in 1576 and designed by G. Alessi. The altar-piece depicting the Pentecost is the work of Cesare Nebbia from Orvieto (16th century), whilst the lateral frescoes are signed by Marcello Leopardi from the Marches region (1795). The so-called Baptistry Chapel follows

1. Giannicola di Paolo (?): Madonna delle Grazie. 2. Federico Barrocci: Deposition (16th century).

24

with frescoes by Domenico Bruschi (1876). The elegant Renaissance relief work on the far wall is the work of Pietro di Paolo and Andrea da Como (1477). Opposite this chapel, on the third octagonal column of the aisle, is the venerated image of the Madonna of Grace, a work in the Perugian style, attribute to Giannicola di Paolo. At the end of the aisle is the splendid chapel of St. Bernardino of Siena standing behind a curious 15th-century wrought-iron grille. The most important painting in the entire church is located above the altar of this chapel: the Deposition from the Cross by Federico Barocchio. This was painted by order of the Merchants' Guild who owned

the chapel during the period, 1567-1569. Outside the chapel, on the left, is a large painting of the Nativity of Our Lady, thought to be the work of Giulio Cesare Angeli (early 17th century).

Before continuing into the Sacristy, we may note the frescoes painted on the vaulting which constitutes a remarkable anthology of 18th-century Perugian painting; they include the work of Francesco Appiani, V. Monotti, V. Carattoli, C.S. Mariotti, M. Leopardi and D. Sergardi.

Passing through a small 15th-century doorway on the right-hand side of St. Emideo's Chapel (right of the apse), one enters the Sacristy, a large square-shaped room adorned with frescoes by Gian Antonio Pandolfi from Pesaro, dating from around 1578. The Martyrdom of St. Lawrence is depicted in the centre of the vault. From right to left, the corbels bear frescoes of the Arrest of St. Lawrence, St. Lawrence is tortured before martyrdom, St. Lawrence distributing the Church's possessions among the poor, the tyrant demands an explanation from St. Lawrence. Following the same order, the lunettes depict Noah's Ark (with a painting of the sybil Cumana on the corresponding vault section; Noah's drunkeness (the Prophet Elijah on the vault section), Samsom destroys the Temple (the Sybil Dephica on the vault section), the Indolence of Dagon (Daniel in the Lion's Den on the vault section), the Passage of the Ark of the Covenant over Jerico (Sybil Persica on the vault section) and the Conquest of Jerico (David with the head of Goliath on the vault section). The vault section above the large windows which are, unfortunately, virtually illegible, depict Jonah and the Sybil Frigia. The ovals depict the three theological virtues (Faith Hope and Charity) and Justice. The sidewall of the chapel bears monochromatic images of the protective Saints Herculanus and Costanzo. The other wall bears paintings of the Four Doctors of the Church (Gregory, Ambrose, Augustine and Jerome). The bases of the thrones depict episodes from their lives in monochrome work.

The **Museum** is host to works of art belonging to the Cathedral or to the Diocese of Perugia. It contains a large number of parchment manuscripts among which are fragment manuscripts of a 6th-century Evangelistery; two Evangelisteries from the 8th and 9th centuries; an 11th-century Biblical Commentary; a Breviary from Maastricht (12th century); a 13th-century French missal; another small Missal dating from the second half of the 1200's originating from St. John of Acri with miniatures by an artist of the Venetian school; a group of 15th-century Antiphonaries, illustrated with miniature work which combines Giottesque elements, Martin-ian motifs and the French style of painting.

Among the paintings exhibited, besides the tryptych by Meo da Siena, there is a Madonna by Andrea Vanni and a tryp-tych by Agnolo Gaddi; there is also a splendid altar-piece by Luca Signorelli, painted for the Chapel of Bishop Vagnucci in 1484. Umbrian painting is represented by a Pietà by Bartolomeo Caporali (who also painted — in collaboration with his brother Giapeco — the miniatures of a late-15th century missal); a fresco of the Perugian school; and altar-piece by Pompeo Cocchi; a large canvas after the style of Girolamo Danti, commisioned by the Masons and Capernters Guilds of Perugia during the second half of the 16th century.

In the room opposite, there are vestments, silver-work and a rare 13th-century faldstool.

On the left, we findt the entrance of the **Graduate Room** in which university degrees were conferred.

Inside, we can see three frescoes: the one on the far wall depicts Pope John XXII between the Emperors Charles IV and Sigismond I; to the left, we see symbolic figures of canon and civil law; on the right, there is an allegorical painting of Medicine next to St. Catherine of Alex-

1. Berto di Giovanni: Banner (detail) (16th century). 2. Giovanni Baglione: The Stoning of St. Stephen (17th century). 3. Arnolfo di Cambio: Head of an Acolyte (13th century).

andria, the patron-saint of Study. This is probably the work of an artist from Assisi who was active during the first decades of the 12th century. The other two frescoes, as well as the illustrations of the Judges Baldo and Bartolo have been much re-painted, probably during the 19th century.

On the far left, one can look down onto the first courtyard of the Presbytery with three terraces dating back to the first half of the 15th century. A total of three papal conclaves took place in the Presbytery fo St. Lawrence (1216, 1265 and 1285).

The cloister also provides access to the *Domenican Library* with its great wealth of manuscripts and around 7,000-8,000 volumes.

The Great Fountain

The famous Great Fountair stand at the centre of the mair square. It was built as a monumen to mark the success of a public in itiative, the completion of the aqueduct which carried water from Monte Pacciano directly into the main square. This project had beer discussed as early as 1254. In 1277 the construction of the aqueduct under the supervision of Fra Bevignate, was the Commune's prime consideration. The Fountain wa: erected in a relatively short time

1. *A miniatured Antiphonary of the 14th century.* 2. *The Great Fountain (12th century).*

(1277-78) even though the water actually reached it a few years later. The architect and director of the works was Fra Bevignate; the hydraulic system was designed by Boninsegna da Venezia and the decorative sculptures were executed by Nicola and Giovanni Pisano. It is often difficult to distinguish between the work of these two individuals. Critics in general tend to attribute to Nicola those panels (most of the months, Adam and Eve, Romulus and Remus, Rea Silvia, Goliath and Samson and Aesope's Fables) and those images on the corners (Perugia, St. Peter, St. Paul and the Baptist) in which the influence of Classicism is more explicit with its controlled and compact solidity of forms. The work of Giovanni is characterized by a more accentuated linear tension and a stronger individuality of expression (Lake Trasimeno, the Chiusi area, Rome, the Roman Church, the two clerics, St. Bernard, Herman of Sassoferrato, Salome and Theology, among the corner statues, and the Eagles, Astronomy, Philosophy and Rhetoric, among the panels). In this period, Giovanni was on the threshold of his most original and mature

period which was to culminate in his great decorative undertaking in the Cathedral of Siena. As for the group of bronze female figures which crowns the upper basin of the fountain, be they represents a sublime expression of plastic sensibility and an extraordinarty composural harmony. The artistic perfection of the monument by no means detracts from its political and symbolic significance. Indeed, the

1. The Great Fountain. 2. The Great Fountain: the panels of the lower basin.

Fountain, besides marking the urban renewal and extension of the piazza, was intended to present an image of a city at the height of its political and cultural power, both internally and externally. It is a true reflection of the society which conceived and built it, bringing together themes from both civil and religious culture (the alliance of Guelph Perugia with Rome was of both religious and political significance) and uniting both sacred and profane elements demonstrating the possibility of riconciliation between Man and Divinity, between religion and history. The fountain which we admire today was accurately restored in 1948-49.

The monument is composed of two polygon-shaped marble basins — one placed above the other.

The lower basin comprises twenty-five sections, each of which is divided into two panels. Beginning from the side facing the Prior's Palace, the illustrations are as follows: I. January: a man seated by a fire holding a plate of chicken and a goblet; a woman, also by the fire-side, holding a bread-cake and a jug; II. February: a man fishing; a man carrying fish; III. March: a man removing a thorn from his foot; a man pruning trees; IV. April: a young man with a coronet of flowers and a girl carrying a basket of fruit; V. May: a horseman holding a bouquet of flowers; a lady with a falcon on her wrist; VI. June: the figure of a man harvesting the grain; a man scything the hay; VII. July: a man beating the grain; a man winnowing; VIII. August: a man and a woman picking fruit; IX. September: a man pressing grapes in a vat; another man carrying a basket of grapes on his shoulders; X. October: a man pouring wine into a cask next to another who is shifting a cask; XI. November: a man at the plough and another sewing seed; XII. December: a man killing the pig next to another man who is in the process of transporting it. Note that each month is accompanied by its appropriate sign of the zodiac. XIII. A griffin (symbol of Perugia) and a lion (emblem of the Guelph party); XIV. Grammar and Dialectics; XX. Rhetoric and Arithmat-

2

ic; XVI. Geometry and Music; XVII. Astronomy and Philosopy; XVIII. Two Eagles (above the one on the right is the signature of Giovanni Pisano); XIX. the Original Sin and the Banishment from the Garden of Eden; XX. Samson and the Lion, Samson and Delilah; XXI. A Lion looking at a man who is beating her cubs (Si vis ut timeat leo, verbera catulum = if you wish the Lion to fear you, beat her young); XXII. David hurls the stone and Goliath falls; XXIII. Romulus and Remus interrogate the birds; XXIV. The She-wolf with the twins and a female figure with a cage in her hand (Rea Silvia?), the original of which is in the Gallery; finally, XXV. the Wolf and the Crane; the Wolf and the lamb.

The statues on the upper basin, beginning on the side facing Corso Vannucci, are as follows: I. Perugia, represented by a *woman* holding the horn-of-plenty; II. Lake Trasimeno, personified as a woman holding a fish; III. St. Herculanus; IV. The traitor priest who revealed Perugia's inability of defence to Totila, after which the city was defeated and Bishop Herculanus martyred; V. St. Bernard and St. Marius; VI. St. John the Baptist; VII. Soloman; VIII. David; IX. Salome; X. Moses; XI. Matthew of Correggio, Podestà of Perugia with the symbol of his authority, the sceptre and gloves; XII. St. Michael the Archangel; XIII. Euliste, the mythical founder of Perugia; XIV. Melchizedek (19th century); XV. Herman of Sassoferrato, Captain of the People, also with the symbolic sceptre and gloves; XVI. Victory; XVII. St. Peter; XVIII. The Roman Church; XIX. Rome dressed in the garbs of a Queen (a copy of the original which is preserved in the Gallery); XX. Theology; XXI. St. Paul; XXII. A monk of St. Lawerence's Order; XXIV. A woman holding a bale of corn, presonification of the Chiugi area, a fertile zone in the contado of Perugia.

The small bronze basin is dated 1277 and is the work of the Perugian sculptor Rosso. It is sustained by a group of three female figures (possibly the three Theological Virtues) attributed to Giovanni Pisano.

The lower cornice of the second basin bears a carved latin inscription welcoming the passer-by and giving him information regarding the authors and date of the monument.

Opposite the Priors' Palace in the **Notaries' Palace** which was built between 1438 and 1446 when the old seat of the Notaries' association, near to the Cathedral, was demolished. It is Gothic in style like the nearby Priors' Palace. Between the two lower mullioned-windows there is the coat-of-arms of the Notaries' Guild: a griffin above and ink-stand. When via Pinella was opened in 1591 the north wing of the building was demolished.

The **Bishop's Palace** also faces onto the square with a façade dating from the second half of the 13th century; the ashlarwork door dates from the second half of the 18th century and bears a landscape in relief.

Other buildings of a later epoch also overlook the piazza such as the attractive Palazzo Friggeri built upon the foundations of an older structure, to a design by Pietro Carattoli who also made its monumental staircase (18th century).

The Merchant's Guild: the Audience Room, detail of the carvedwood decoration (15th century).

1

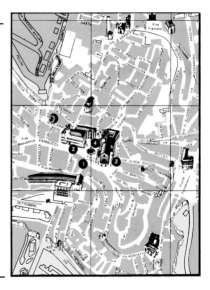

Alongside the Priors' Palace, following Corso Vannucci, we first come across the **Merchants' Guild** and **Exchange Building**. The Merchants' and Exchange Guilds were the most powerful in the city. Two members of the Merchants' and one of the Exchange Guild had the right to be repeatedly elected as priors so

that representative of these two associations were always present among the top levels of the political and administrative management of the town. With the general aristocratic take-over (from the 15th century onwards), the guilds were transformed from free associations open to all trade members to institutions which were exclusively reserved for the nobility (1670).

The Merchants' Guild

In 1390, the seat of the Merchants' Guild resided in the Priors' Palace; here, it sponsored the elegant decorations in carved wood which adorn the walls of the Audience Room (poplar and walnut) during the first four decades of the 15th century, although it is probable — given the complexity of the project — that it was not completed until the middle of this century. The rarity of the decorative type, seldom found in Italy, leads us to conclude that its author was of nordic origins. Regarding this point, there is evidence that a certain Nicolò Tedesco was active in Perugia in 1450 during the construction of an altar in the New Chapel of the

Palace. The splendid carved bench is the work of the Perugian, Costanzo di Mattiolo (1462); it was placed in the Merchants' Guild Room in 1855, after in had been acquired by the Notaries' Guild. Enrolment registers from the years 1323, 1356 and 1599, illustrated with miniatures are preserved in the archives. The vault next to the main one bears frescoes by Domenico Bruschi of Perugia (1898-1899).

The Exchange Guild

(Collegio del Cambio)

The money-changers' guild, together with the merchants' guild, was the most important trade guild in Perugia. Probably existing as far back as the beginning of the thirteenth century, it was mainly concerned with the circulation of money, loans and money exchange. In the earliest period, the guild did not have a permanent seat. It was not until the 15th century that it established itself in its present location in Palazzo dei Priori, or to be more precise, on the site once occupied by the church of S.Giovanni del Mercato. Work to expand

and renovate the new premises began in 1452 and was completed in 1457. The work was carried out by the architect BARTOLOMEO DI MATTIOLO from Torgianó and the stonecutter LODOVICO D'ANTONIBO.

Visitors enter the college from the **sala dei legisti** (Legist' Room), whose wood ornamentation was completed between 1615 and 1621 by GIAMPIETRO ZUCCARI, an artist from the Marche, assisted by GIOVANNI DI ANDREA and ANTONIO DI MENICO.

Visitors may then go into the **sala dell'udienza** (Audience Room) where auditors exercised their jurisdiction. The room was completely decorated between 1490 and 1500. The first thing to be completed was the woodwork (tribunal, back, bench, postergale), by the Florentine artist DOMENICO DEL TASSO (1490-1492). The next works to be completed were the precious terracotta portraying *Justice* (lunette above the tribunal), attributed to BENEDETTO DA MAIANO and the entrance door inlaid by ANTONIO DA MERCATELLO (1501). The last work commissioned was the pulpit by the Flemish artist AN-

TONIO MASI, who was assisted by EUSEBIO DEL BASTONE (1562).

On 26 January 1496, PIETRO VANNUCCI, known as IL PERUGINO, was commissioned to decorate the whole interior with paintings. Although the final receipt of payment was not issued until 1507, the works were probably completed in the period between 1498 and 1500.

The decoration on the vault consists of allegorical representations (*Moon, Mercury, Mars, Saturn, Jupiter, Venus, Apollo*) framed by grotesque ornamental motifs. *Cato* is portrayed on the right side of the entrance. On the left side, in the first lunette, below the personifications of Prudence and Justice, there are six characters from the classical world: *Fabius Maximus, Socrates, Numa Pompilius, Furius Camillus, Pittacus and Trajan*. On the dividing pilaster appears the self-portrait of Perugino. In the second lunette we see *Fortitude* and *Temperance* with six other heroes: *Lucius Sicinius, Leonida, Horatio Colclite, Publius Scipio, Pericles, Cincinnata*.

On the back wall there is the *Transfiguration* and the *Nativity*.

Represented in the lunette of the remaining wall are six *Sibyls*, six *Prophets* and *Benedictory Eternity*. The pilaster which follows bears a plaque with the writing «Anno Salut. MD», the date the works were finished.

The complex iconographic cycle, acompanied by lengthy explanations, reflects the thought of the Perugian humanist Francesco Maturanzio, a lecturer at the

1. Pietro Perugino: Ancient personages and allegorical figures (16th century). 2. Pietro Perugino: Mercory (16th century).

35

University and secretary of the Decemvirs, who had proposed a decidedly «Ficiniano» topic for the 'stories': man who draws near to God through the incarnation of the Word, the harmony of the world reached through the reconciliation between classical studies and Christian piety» (V. Zabughin, 1924).

The wall containing the *Nativity* and the *Transfiguration* is where we can most clearly see the hand of Perugino. Examples of extremely high quality may also be found, however, in the lunette with the *Sibyls* and the *Prophets*, where some have suggested (but mistakenly) a contribution by the young Raphael. It is here that may observe »Perugino at his best, the liveliest and most inspired Perugino who paints in full inventive freedom». In fact, the beautiful composition of the two groups placed in juxtaposition, in such great musical harmony, was executed by freely transposing the cartoons on the fresh plaster with rapid, approximate incisions that were directly traced with a pointed instrument, and over which the artist painted broad areas... In the landscape as well, the small, dark-coloured, parallel brushstrokes on a green or brown background create a great contrast of light, without precedents in Perugino's art (P.Scarpellini, 1984). The vault was mainly completed by the artist's collaborators: the names suggested are GIOVANNI DI FRANCESCO CIAMBELLA, known as IL FANTASIA, ANDREA D'ASSISI, known as L'INGEGNO, and ROBERTO DA MONTEVARCHI.

A small door beneath the lunette with the Sibyls and Prophets leads in-

to the *cappella of S.Giovanni Battista*. This chapel, which corresponds to the old church of S.Giovanni del Mercato, was rebuilt in 1509 by the Lombard architect GASPERINO DI PIETRO.

The woodwork was done by ANTONIO BENCIVENNI DA MERCATELLO (1509).

In 1512 Mariano di Ser Austerio was commissioned to do the altar front. In 1513 GIANNICOLA DI PAOLO was assigned the task of decorating the vault. Shortly afterwards (1515) he was also commissioned to paint the frescoes on the walls and the altarpiece.

A new contract was stipulated in 1518, whereas the final payment dates back to 1528-29.

Not far beyond the Exchange Building, on the left, one can turn into Via Mazzini, opened in 1547 and constructed by order of the Delegate Cardinal Tiberius Crispo. It was designed by Galeazzo Alessi who also designed the façade of the church of **St. Mary of the People** (no. 9) which is today used for secular functions. At the end of this street, we find ourselves in Piazza Matteotti.

During the Mediaeval era, this was the 'Piazza of the Wall', as it was built upon arches resting against the Etruscan Wall; it was also known as the Piazza Piccola in relation to the Piazza Grande of which we have already spoken. These two main piazzas were linked by a series of 'folds' which have now disappeared following modern reconstruction works. This piazza was host to the herb market and possessed several monuments which have either been destroyed or removed: in front of the Old University doorway, there stood the beginnings of a portico by Valentino Martelli (1591) which was never completed; its elegant central arch can today be seen infront of the Church of St. Francis al Prato. Above this arch, there stood a bronze statue of Pope Sextus V which was melted down by the French in 1798 in order to make coins; a 15th-century fountain was situated at the centre of the piazza.

1. Pietro Perugino: Self portrait (16th century). 2. Giannicola di Paolo: Chapel of St. John the Baptist (detail) (16th century).

The Old University Building (Palazzo dell'Università Vecchia)

The **Old University Building** marks the Western confines of the piazza. In 1266, Perugia either already had or was certainly in the process of planning a *Studium*; in 1308 — although university activity had in fact existed for sometime — Pope Clement granted Perugia the status of *Studium generale*. The building we see today dates from the second half of the 15th century. It is composed of a first floor of ogival gothic arches and a second floor with Renaissance-style cross windows. Sextus IV instituted the University's headquarters there in 1483 and they remained here until 1811. Today, the building accomodates the town's Magistrates Court. Long ago, the Hospital of St. Mary of Mercy had several workshops in the building; the architrave of no. 31 bears the hospital's coat-of-arms sustained by two griffins and dated 1472.

The Captain of the People's Palace

To the left, stands the **Captain of the People's Palace**, erected between 1470 and 1480 and designed by the Lombard masters, Gasperino di Antonio and Leone di Matteo. Note the fact that the door is similar in type to the side-door of the Priors's Palace. It also has a fine loggia supported by consoles. The third floor was demolished after the earthquake of 1741. Today, this building also contains court offices.

Continuing along to no. 18-18a, two archways lead us to a renovated 14th-century loggia and the terrace which accomodates the town's indoor market (1932). From here, we can enjoy the splendid panorama of the Assisi Valley.

The Butchers' and Woolmakers' Guilds held there meetings in the area.

37

The Church of Jesus
(Chiesa del Gesù)

The **Church of Jesus** is at the beginning of Via Alessi. It was built on the site of the former church of St. Andrew and of the St. Salvatore. Works on the church were begun in 1562. It was consecrated in 1571 and was extended around 1620 when the transept was added. After the suppression of the Jesuit Order in 1775,

1. The Captain of the People's Palace. 2. Emblem of the Hospital of Mercy.

the church was entrusted to the Order of St. Barnabus.

The façade, originally completed as far as the cornice of the first floor, was finished in 1934 following a model found in a painting by Pietro Malambra which can be seen in the Umbrian National Gallery.

The interior has a nave and two aisles. The nave is composed of carved gold-plated lacunas by Girolamo Bruscatelli and Marco Pace from Perugia (16th century). On either side of the sumptuous main-altar, built in 1613 on African-black columns taken from the Church of Sant'Angelo, are two canvases by the Perugian artist, Stefano Amadei, depicting the Nativity and the Adoration of the Magi (17th century). The transept vault is completely covered with frescoes depicting the story of Joshua, painted by Andrea Carlone from Genoa (1656). The Sacristy, where the famous Madonna of the Cherry Tree was once preserved, today contains numerous pieces of valuable furniture in walnut, dating from the 18th century. The vault bears a fresco by Andrea Pozzi (18th century).

The church is surmounted by three oratories which, in their turn, are placed one above the order, forming a kind of tower corresponding to the apse. From the north aisle, a staircase leads to the Oratory of the Nobles (1596) which has frescoes by Girolamo Martelli and Cesare Sermei (17th century). Beneath this, according to a strict scale of social class, is the Oratory of the Artisan Congregation (1603) with frescoes by Anton Maria Fabrizi, G. Andrea Carlone and Cesare Sermei and two large lunettes by Paolo Gismondi (the Nativity of the Virgin) and Pietro Montanini (the Presentation in the Temple), both 18th-century Perugian artist. Again underlining the rigid adherence to class rules, the entrance to the third Oratory, that of the peasants (1603) is outside the church, in Via Augusta, a road which crosses Via Alessi. This is decorated with simple ornamental motifs by Pier Francesco Colombati (1746), a modest imitatore of Pietro Carattoli. On the left, at the far end of the Piazza, the suggestive Via Volte della Pace begins. This is composed of a long portico of pointed arches built during the 13th century along the path of the Etruscan wall. This road leads into Via Bontempi which we follow briefly, turning left into Via Raffaello, at the end of which we find ourselves in Piazza Raffaello.

The Church of St. Severo

The **Church of St. Severo** is situated in this piazza. Its present-day form originates from the 1750's. It was the seat of the Camaldolite Order from the beginning of the 11th century up to 1935, when it was taken over by the lay clergy. The interior follows the Neoclassical architectural model and has frescoes by Guglielmo Ascanio of whom a signed and dated sketch is preserved in the sacristy. The south arm of the transept, which forms a spacious chapel, contains a canvas by Francesco Appiani (1760), depicting Jesus Christ in glory placing a crown on the head of Blessed Michael the Hermit in company of SS. Scolastica and Antony of Padua. On the opposing altar, enclosed within an 18th-century

2

tabernacle of gold-plated wood, is a figure of the Virgin of Sassoferrato (a copy of the original which is preserved in the parish centre). Above the main-altar is a large canvas by Stefano Amadei (1632 circa) dipicting the Virgin and Child among a company of Saints (Benedict, Romualdo, Severo, Andrew, Lucy and Catherine of Alexandria). The altar of the north arm has a painting of the Immaculate Conception by a disciple of Francesco Appiani (18th century). Beside the church is a 15th-century chapel which is a remnant of a renovation which took place in that period. The far wall bears the only certain work by Raphael to remain in Perugia. The upper section which is the one attributed to Raphael (1505-08), depicts the Trinity with SS. Marius, Placido and Benedict Abbot; on the left hand side are SS. Romualdo, Benedict the Martyr and Giovanni the monk. The lower section was painted by the Perugino in 1521; it shows SS. Scolastica, Jerome, John the Evangelist, Gregory Magno, Boniface and Martha. At the centre, within a niche, is a statue of the Madonna and Child in terracotta dating from the late 1400's. The fresco was restored in 1976.

From Piazza Raffaello, we proceed along Via dell'Aquila; turning left, we enter Piazza Biordo Michelotti; crossing this piazza, after a brief descent, we come to Piazza Rossi Scotti. For a short period of time, this piazza was the site of an imposing fortress which was destroyed when the Abbot of Monmaggiore was banished from the city (1375-76); all that remains of the fortress are the huge arches which support a section of the wall. From this position, we can enjoy one of the many beautiful panoramas which Perugia has to offer. To the left, we can see the Porta Sant'Angelo quarter of the city (covering the area from the Foreign University to the Monastery of Monteripido); on the right, we see the bell-tower of Santa Maria Nuova, attributed to Galeazzo Alessi, and the Medioeval wall to the St. Antony

quarter. Descending the steps of Via delle Prome (on the left), we arrive in Via Bartolo, directly in front of the Etruscan wall, with the famous Arch of Augustus a little further on.

On the corner of Via delle Prome stands the **Church of St. Angelo della Pace** (the Angel of Peace) the construction of which was ordered by the delegate Cardinal Tiberius Crispo. Traditionally, it was been attributed to Galeazzo Alessi but modern scholars have suggested that it was designed by Raffaello da Montelupo. It was originally a loggia but was subsequently closed and transformed into an oratory. The adjacent building was the original seat of the Academy of Design.

The huge building on the corner

1. View. 2. The Etruscan well.

40

between Piazza Rossi Scotti and Via delle Prome is the Palace of the Constable of the Cavalry, now the seat of the **Augusta Communal Library**, founded by Prospero Podiani in the 1580's. The Library possesses a conspicuous collection of volumes (early printed books, 16th-century works) and many precious manuscripts.

Following Via del Sole, we descend into Piazza Danti. Between this piazza and Piazza Piccino (no. 48), we come across the **Etruscan Well**. It is cylindrical in shape and the basin is composed of circular ashlar work. It is 35 metres deep with a maximum diameter of 5.60 metres. The exact date of the well is difficult to estimate: 400-200 B.C.? The large building on the shorter side of the Piazza is the **Turreno Theatre**, built in 1819 to a design by Alessandro Arienti; it was renovated in 1926 and 1953.

2

41

2

Itinerary

The Etruscan Arch - the Church of St. Augustine - the Convent of the Beata Colomba - the Convent of St. Agnes - the Temple of St. Michael the Archangel - the Church of St. Matthew - the Monastery of Monteripido.

From the left side of Piazza Danti, we turn into Via V. Rocchi, nick-named 'Via Vecchia' because of its antiquity. It was probably one of the five principal roads linking the 'borghi' (quarters) to the Piazza of the Commune. Its parallel, Via Bartolo, was opened in 1378. At the level of no. 34 is the former *Oradino College*, founded in 1582 by Polidoro Oradini to train young men for priesthood. It has an elegantly designed 16th-century doorway. At a certain point, we enter Piazza Ansidei with its attractive Palazzo Ansidei (18th century). At nos. 29-31 Via V. Rocchi, the façade of the ancient parish church of St. Donato can still be seen.

The Etruscan Arch

(Arco Etrusco)

Continuing to the end of Via F. Rocchi, we arrive at the **Etruscan Arch** (or **Arch of Augustus**), one of the seven or eight doorways of the *urbs vetus*, whose wall was 2.9 kilometres in length. Its imposing structure has always attracted great admiration. In a document dating

1036, it is referred to as the *Porta Pulchra* (= the Beautiful Door) but it had been thus defined since the late 7th century. Francesco Suriano, a Franciscan who lived in the 15th century, described the walls of the Egyptian pyramid as being «all covered with large life-like slabs of stone... each fitting into the other *as in the city door of Via Vecchia in Perugia*, with marvellous artifice

without mortar, each bound to the other...».

The Arch affords a frontal view of Piazza Fortebracci. It consists of two trapezoidal towers with an ornamental façade in the centre. The barrel-vault is corniced by two concentric armillas and by a moulded cavetto with a frieze of triglyphs surmounting tapered Ionic columns and metopes with rounded shields; above this is an upper level consisting of a open arch between two Ionic columns; on top, is a Renaissance style loggia (16th century). On the two concentric borders of

the lower arch are the words «*Augusta Perusia*» and, inscribed on the cornice below the frieze, «*Colonia Vibia*».

The fountain on the left was completed in 1621.

Piazza Fortebracci was built by order of the delegate Cardinal Marino Grimani in 1536. Apart from the Etruscan Arch, it is dominated by the imposing Palazzo Antinori, subsequently named after Gallenga Stuart, which is now the headquarters of the **Italian University for Foreigners** which opened in 1926.

It is an attractive 18th-century building in laterite stone, built by Pietro Carattoli to a design by the Roman architect, Francesco Branchi (1740-1758). The interior is decorated with frescoes attributed

1. Fountain of the Etruscan Arch (1621). 2. The Etruscan Arch.

to Giuli and Carattoli; the third floor accomodates a series of canvases commissioned by Girolamo Antinori in 1762. The building was enlarged, preserving, however, its original style, during the period 1935-37.

Right of the Arch, is the **Church of St. Fortunato**, probably of paleo-Christian or high-Mediaeval origins. In 1163, it was listed among the dependencies of the Cathedral of Perugia. Without doubt, it was a parish church in 1285. In its present form, it has existed since 1633 when it was rebuilt by Silvestrine monks who had been transferred here definitively after the construction of the Rocca Paolina. The façade still reveals the structure of the Mediaeval church: it has a double-sloping roof and a trapezoidal bell-tower. It is an aisless church and contains wooden gold-plated altars with French-style statues, some of which are by Leonardo Scaglia. The painting at the far end of the Chior, depicting the Madonna, St. Fortunato and St. Gregory, is the work of the Perugian artist, Scilla Pecennini. It was originally placed above the main-altar, now demolished, the decoration of which was executed by Bino Sozi in 1584.

If we continue along Corso Garibaldi (former Via della Lungara), we enter a typical 'popular' quarter, a lively and animated part of the city. During the Mediaeval age, it housed a mainly artisan population and it is a characteristic example of a new quarter which grew up outside the city walls.

1. Gallenga's Palace (18th century). 2. The Church of St. Augustine: Interior (18th century).

quarter of Perugia during the period 1256-60 and a Gothic church was built of which only a few chapels remain. The interior, as seen today, was rebuilt between the 18th and 19th centuries by Stefano Canzacchi di Amelia and is Neoclassical in style.

Some Gothic chapels are to be found in the northern part of the nave and at the beginning of the transept. The second chapel to the left of the nave contains a fresco depicting the Crucifixion by Pellino di Vannuccio (1377); the third chapel contains another fresco — a Madonna on the throne between SS. Joseph and Jerome — by an early 16th century artist. The fourth chapel has late 16th century decorations on its lunettes painted by Giovan Battista Lombardelli, an artist from the Marches region of Italy.

To the right of the nave, the first chapel is ornamented by Francesco di Guido di Viorio of Settignano in the Renaissance style (16th century). Here, we can admire a Madonna of Grace attributed to Giannicola di Paolo. In the second gothic chapel, there are two large canvases by Arrigo Fiammingo dated 1515 (Christ and St. Andrew) and 1560 (the Martyrdom of St. Catherine).

At the head of the transept, we find the remains of a chapel originating from the previous gothic structure. In the chapel on the right, there are frescoes attributed to Allegretto Nazi and Piero di Puccio of Orvieto (1398). In the south wing of the transept, is a Deposition from the Cross dating back to the second half of the 14th century. The wooden choir in the apse is the work of Braccio d'Agnolo, perhaps based on a drawing by the Perugino. The Perugino also painted the large altar-piece, today partially

The Church of St. Augustine

A short distance further ahead, we reach Piazza Domenico Lupatelli (a citizen of Perugia who died in the failed undertaking of the Bandiera brothers), which is dominated by the façade of the **church of St. Augustine**. The lower gothic section is overlaid with pink and white slabs forming the chequered pattern so typical of Perugia (cf. the Church of St. Mary of Monteluce, the Church of St. Juliana etc.). It has twin-doors. Its laterite upper section is Mannerist in style and is attributed to Bino Sozi (16th century).

The Augustinians established themselves in the Sant'Angelo

tar, made by Marco Pace of Perugia to a design by Bino Sozi (1586), is host to a panel by Raffaellino del Colle (1563). The Sacristy contains perspective decorations by Pietro Carattoli (1762 circa) and paintings by Francesco Appiani. Above the altar is the processional banner by Giovanni Antonio Scaramuccia (1625) which depicts the Virgin and Child between SS. Augustine, Francis and Domenic. Beneath the Oratory, in rooms which, unfortunately, are not open to the public but which, because of their importance, should be pointed out, was the ancient seat of the hospice run by the monks. It is a huge ambient with cross-vaulting and 14th-century frescoes, among them, a Crucifixion attributed to the Maestro of Paciano; the far wall bears frescoes of the Crucifixion with the prostrate Virgin supported by St. John and Mary Magdalen, who is embracing the cross: this is a work of the Perugian school dating from the first half of the 16th century.

preserved in the Umbrian National Gallery.

Next to the Church is the **Oratory of the Augustinian Brotherhood**, built in 1317. We reach the interior via a passage containing frescoes by Francesco Appiani. Inside, we find one of the richest and most interesting ambients to be produced during the proto-Baroque period in Perugia. The vault is made of carved, gold-plated wood and the stalls are the work of the French artists, Charles d'Amuelle and Monsù Filippe. The paintings on the wall depicting episodes from the lives of Jesus and SS. Phillip and James were realised between 1618 and 1630 and are the work of Giulio Cesare Angeli of Perugia with the exception of the last three on the right which are by Bernardino Gagliardo of Città di Castello (1656). The paintings on the vault are by Mattia Batini (1700). The al-

The Convent of St. Catherine

Following Corso Garibaldi up to no. 179, we come to the Benedictine **Convent of St. Catherine**, built around 1547 to a design by Galeazzo Alessi. Its construction was sponsored by the Convent of St. Juliana whose sisters were its proprietors, having built it with the intention of moving there. It was probably the seat of the Convent of

1. The Oratory of St. Augustine (17th century). 2. The Church of St. Catherine: Interior (18th century).

46

St. Clare which had been established in the 1380's. In 1647 it was taken over by the nuns of St. Catherine Vecchia who solemnly established themselves there in 1649. Inside the church, the vault bears frescoes depicting episodes from the life of St. Catherine of Alexandria by Mattia Batini and canvases by Benedetto Bandiera (St. Ursula and the Virgins; the Mystical Marriage of St. Catherine; the Crucifixion; the Descent of the Holy Spirit) and also by Batini (the Immaculate Conception).

The Convent of the Beata Colomba

At no. 191 is the **Convent of the Beata Colomba** (second order Dominican nuns), established, after the merger of this convent with that of St. Thomas (1940), together taking over the former Convent of Charity. Inside, there is a reconstruction of the Beata's cell (she was a mystic Dominican tertiary who died in Perugia in 1501) which contains relics of the same. Here, we find a suggestive painting of

Christ on the Cross attributed to Spagna (late 15th century). The church's left-hand altar has a canvas by L. Caselli which is an early 19th-century copy of the Disbelief of St. Thomas by Giannicola di Paolo, today preserved in the Umbrian National Gallery; above the grille behind the main altar, there is a painting by Francesco Appiani which was taken from the Monastery of St. Thomas. The vault was decorated by Nicola Giuli of Perugia (18th century).

Bordering the convent is a stretch of Via dello Spernadio which is interrupted by the Mediaeval **Porta Sperandio**. This low arch, in alternated travertine and sandstone is supported by two quoins which also form the piers. The arch bears in 1329 'porta ista restaurata fuit' (this door was restored). On either side we can admire the mediaeval walls of the city built in a combination of sandstone, calcareous and travertine rock. Proceeding forward from the Sperandio arch, we come to the former Convent of St. Sperandio, supposedly established in 1262 by Abess Santuccia of Gubbio on land donated by Sis-

ter Sperandia Sperandei, also from Gubbio. Suppressed in 1799, it was used as a private villa. The external door still bears the inscription «Spera in Deo 1696». Nearby, a small convent was built by the Order of St. Sperandio, possibly as early as the 13th century; of this convent, there remains part of the Cloister to be seen in no. 6, Via Sperandio (Casa Mori).

The Convent of St. Agnes

Following Corso Garibaldi, we turn left into Via S. Agnese which leads us to the above mentioned **monastery**; it was the seat of the Poor Clares during the year 1329-30; in the period 1428-30, it was passed into the hands of Franciscan Tertiary nuns who remained there up to 1911 when it was again taken over by the Poor Clares. The convent's church (17th century) contains canvases by Perugian artists of the period: Bassotti (The Falgellation of Christ) and Angeli (The Madonna and Jesus Christ in Glory with St. Francis offering them roses, dated 1615; St. Agnes and other figures). In one of the arches of the Choir, on either side of a woodern crucifix, there are paintings of Our Lady and St. John the Evangelist; in the intrados, there are paintings of St. Sebastian, the Eternal Father and St. Rocco, attributed to Eusebio da S. Giorgio (1519). An internal chapel, which is nonetheless open to visitors has a fresco by Perugino depicting Our Lady of Grace between St. Antony Abbot and St. Antony of Padua (1522).

The Temple of St. Michael the Archangel

Via del Tempio takes us directly to the paleo-Christian **Church of St. Michael the Archangel**. Its origins go as far back as the 5th and 6th centu-

1. The Sperandio Gate. 2. The Convent of St. Agnes: Pietro Perugino, The Crowned Madonna(16th century). 3. The Temple of St. Michael the Archangel.

ries; in 1036, it became a dependency of the Cathedral Charter. The central plan of the building is similar in type to the Church of St. Stephen Rotonda in Rome with four chapels facing onto the ambulatory, each following the Greek Cross model. The central space is separated from the ambulatory by a circle of sixteen Roman Corinthian columns which support the tiburio, the materials used for these arches were obviously plundered from elsewhere due to the diversity of height and type of marble; the coussinets above the roman Corinthian style capitals give evidence of the Byzantine influence originating from Ravenna. The saddle-roof is supported by ribs resting on elegant corbels; these, together with the door-way, are of the Gothic period. Following the course of the ambulatory from the right of the entrance, we come across the following: a 14th-century fresco; the Baptistry with frescoes by a 15th-century Umbrian artist; the Madonna del Verde, a fresco originally situated in the cathedral which is a local work dating from the early 13th century, placed above a Roman tablet of the period of Marcus Aurelius. The altar is composed of a marble slab set above a drum.

On leaving the Temple, immediately on the right, we descend a small staircase which leads us to the **Tower of porta Sant'Angelo**. This is largest of the mediaeval city doors and was built in several different phases during the early 14th century; the interior reveals the wall of ashlar-work

ed to the monks of St. John the Baptist by the Canons of the Cathedral; the church was consecrated in 1273. Inside, the nave is subdivided into two parts. It is overhung by cross-vaulting resting on six huge columns which jut of the wall. The far wall has a large trilobated window and is adorned by important frescoes painted by a 13th-century Umbrian artist. They depict the Ascension of Christ, the Twelve Apostles, St. Matthew the Apostle and St. Francis of Assisi, the enthroned Madonna and Child with a Saint, probably St. Basil. The lateral walls bear votive frescoes dating from the 13th and 14th centuries. Of particular interest is a painting of the enthroned Madonna and Child with a Saint, probably St. Basil. The lateral walls bear votive frescoes dating from the 13th and 14th centuries. Of particular interest is a painting of the enthroned Madonna among the saints which is dated 1348 and was undeoubtedly executed by a Perugian artist. Also of interest is a St. Leonard with a kneeling congregation.

sandstone; the vault is maade of bricks. In the piers, the slabs of travertine reveal the fluting necessary to accomodate a slide-door. From the exterior, it is easy to distinguish the three phases of construction and the various different materials employed in each: sandstone at the base, calcareous rock in the centre and brick in the upper regions.

The Church of St. Matthew

Beyond the tower, in Via Monteripido, the **Church of St. Matthew of the Armenians** is immediately on our left. In 1272, this site was donat-

1. The Temple of St. Michael the Archangel: Interior. 2. The keep of St. Angelo Gate. 3. The Monastery of Monteripido.

50

The Monastery of Monteripido

Ascending a suggestive uphill-street, bordered on the right by the Stations of the Via Crucis (1633-1636), we arrive at the **Monastery of St. Francis of the Mount** (Monteripido). Among these hills dwelt the Blessed Egidio (+ 1262), one of the first disciples of St. Francis, near to the residence of the Noble Coppoli family and particularly under the 'protection' of Giacomo di Boncorte. In 1276, the latter donated the site on which he had lived including the house, oratory and other buildings, to the Minor friars of the Monastery of St. Francis al Prato in Perugia. From 1290 onwards, we have evidence of an active monastery community. In 1374, Monteripido was donated to Fra Paoluccio Trinci, a promoter of the Franciscan Observants' movement. From this time on, the history of the monastery is linked to that of the Observants who established a prestigious *Studium* for the monks of this Order. St. Bernardino of Siena stayed there several times and St. Giovanni of Capestrano was a novice there.

The church was reconstructed in a modern style by Tommaso Stamigni of Perugia in 1858. The interior, which still contains the chapel erected by Orazio di Bevignate Alessi in 1588 (with 20th-century frescoes), contains a fine wooden cross which is perhaps the work of Eusebio Bastoni (16th century). Backing onto the curve of the apse, is a Choir made in walnut by Girolamo di Ronaldo and Masco Pace between 1571 and 1581. This originally belonged to the Dominican monks. Behind the apse, there is a small chapel which is said to be the cell of the blessed Egidio, containg a much re-painted Crucifix by a 13th-century Umbrian artist. The first of the three cloisters has lunettes bearing much-damaged fres-

coes of the early 17th-century Assisi school. Those on the left are attributed to Anton Maria Fabrizi. The far wall of the refectory has frescoes by an anonimous Mannerist artist of the late 16th century, probably local in origin but including stylistic components characteristic of the Flemish school. On the left, there is a fresco of the Feeding of the Five Thousand; in the centre, the Crucifixion of St. Veronica and, on the right, the Refection of St. Clare.

The Monastery library with its well-preserved decorations and furniture (the library material is now to be found in the Augusta Communal Library), was built to a design by Pietro Carattoli between 1754 and 1790. Carattoli also designed the external architecture and the walnut furniture.

3 Itinerary

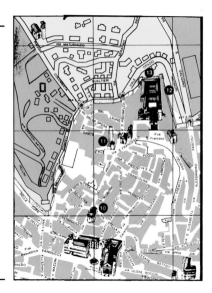

The Church of SS. Severo and Agatha - The Chiesa Nuova - The church of S. Theresa - The Oratory of S. Francis - The Church of St. Francis - The Oratory of St. Bernardino - Monte Morcino Nuovo - The Maestà delle Volte.

The first road to cross Corso Vannucci is Via dei Priori which begins under the great vault of the Priors' Palace. It is a characteristic road, typical of Perugia's historical centre, with openings into suggestive mediaeval side-road and numerous private and religious buildings.

After a brief stretch of this road, we turn into via della Gabbia (of the Cage) which leads back into the Main Piazza (Piazza IV Novembre). This road taken its name from the fact that it was here that condemned prisoners were exhibited to the blood hungry public. From here, we can see a tower which is completely incorporated into the Priors' Palace.

Anonymous 16th century artist: the Feeding of the Five Thousand.

The Church of SS. Severo and Agatha

Continuing along Via dei Priori, we come across the **Church of SS. Severo and Agatha** on our left. It is probable that a pre-existing chapel to St. Agatha stood here; it is known for certain that the church we see today was built by the Commune at the beginning of the 14th century in order to compensate for the permission granted by the ecclesiastical authorities to demolish the church of St. Severo di Piazza in order to extend the Priors' Palace. As early as 1319, the «ecclesia nova Sancti Severi» was spoken of. Inside, there are frescoes dating from around the beginning of the 14th century: on the lefthand wall, the Story of St. Severo after the style of Simone Martini and, on the far wall, the Crucifixion by an artist who was influenced by Pietro Lorenzetti (Maestro di Paciano?). There also numerous votive frescoes. Behind the altar is a polyptych showing Our Lady and Saints, a copy of the panel by Lello da Velleetri, today preserved in the Umbrian National Gallery.

A short way further ahead, we can turn into Via Ritorta for a moment, in order to get an idea of the typical mediaeval streets in the area of Via dei Priori. At no. 22, we note a spiral staircase leading up to a house; at n. 14, there is an arched doorway decorated with gothic

relief work depicting animals; at nos. 1 and 1a, we can see a characteristic mediaeval tower. On the right, there is the Church of the Maestà delle Volte (cf. further on).

At the beginning of Via Ritorta, no. 24 Via dei Priori, there is a fine doorway of a private house which was probably made by Valentino Martelli.

structed on the side of the early-Christian Baptistry of St. Giovanni Rotondo which, in 1618, had been given to the fathers of the Oratory Congregation whose arrival in Perugia (1614) had been solicited by Bishop Napoleon Conitoli. The first stone of this edifice which was to cancel all trace of the former one, was laid in 1626. The project was entrusted to the Roman architect, Paolo Maruscelli, whose design conformed to the dictates regardings architecture prescribed at the Council of Trent. The façade, similar to that of the Church of St. Susanna in Rome, was completed in 1665, whilst the longitudinal body and cross-wing of the church were built between 1627 and 1634. The dome was erected later in 1648.

It is an aisleless church, similar in style to the Church of St. Mary in Vallicella (or Chiesa Nuova) in Rome, and has a vaulted ceiling and side-chapels.

The vault was decorated in 1762 by Francesco Appiani with themes lifted from the Apocalypse of St. John. The chiaroscuro ornamentation is by Nicola Giuli (1762). The penditives of the cupola, with images of the Four Evangelists are by Giovanni Andrea Carlone (1668) who also painted the frescoes in the apse and in the Bigazzini Chapel (1668-69) and in the Chapel of the

The Chiesa Nuova

(New Church)

Continuing along Via dei Priori, on our right, we come to the **New Church of St. Phillip Neri** or **or the Conception**. This church was con-

1. Via Ritorta. 2. The Church of St. Philip Neri or The New Church: Façade (17th century).

Presentation of Mary (second on the left) which is, unfortunately, much re-painted. The paintings in the cupola, depicting the Coronation of Mary, are the work of Francesco Mancini from the Marches region of Italy (1728-1730). The frescoes in the north transept are by the Perugian artists, Giacinto Boccanera and Paolo Brizi (1735); those in the south transept are by Sebastiano Ceccarini of Urbino and Paolo Brizi (1737). The first chapel on the southside (dedicated to the Visitation of Mary) is decorated with frescoes by Vincenzo Monotti and Girolamo Perugini (1776) and has, above the altar, a canvas by Giuseppe Passeri of Rome (1709); the second (the Chapel of the Purification) has frescoes by Bernardino Gagliardi (1649) and was once host to the fine canvas by Andrea Sacchi (1631), today preserved in the Umbrian National Gallery; the third (the Chapel of the Assumption), with frescoes by Anton Maria Fabrizi (1636-1637), was built to a design by Marascelli between 1635 and 1637. Above the altar, there used to be the original of the Assumption by Guido Reni, today in the museum of Lyon (1637 circa). The canvas we see today is the work of Giovan Francesco Romanelli (17th century). The altar of the south transept was designed by Tommaso Stati (1652) and has a copy of an original by Giudo Reni. Behind the main-altar which was also designed by Stati (1645), there hangs a large painting of the Conception of Mary by Pietro da Cortona (1662) with the probable collaboration of his pupils. The curve of the apse contains two paintings depicting St. John and St. Gregory by Pietro Montanini (1674), painted for the Church of St. Philip in memory of the unification of the two parishes of St. John Rotonda

and St. Gregory the Great. The altar of the north transept has a precious bronze crucifix by Pasquale Pasqualini from Vianza (1685). Going back into the nave, the third chapel of the left (dedicated to the Birth of Our Lady), is decorated with frescoes by Anton Maria Fabrizi (1642). Above the altar, there used to be a Nativity by Pietro da Cortona, now in the Umbrian National Gallery. There now hangs a canvas by Simeone Cibur-

ri depicting the Stigmata of St. Francis; the second chapel (of the Presentation of Mary), is adorned with frescoes by Giovanni Andrea Carlone and once displayed a canvas by Luigi Scaramuccia (also in the Gallery) which has now been replaced by a painting by Ulisse Ribustinni; the first chapel (of the Annunciation), with frescoes by Vincenzo Monotti and Girolamo Perugini (1766) has, above the altar, a fine work by Francesco Trevisani (1710).

The Sacristy has a ceiling decorated by V. Carattoli and F. Appiani (18th century). It contains an oil painting by Vincenzo Pellegrini, alias the «Pittor Bello», representing the Conception with Archangel Michael and Mary Magdalen together with two small copper figures by Pietro Montanini (unfortunately stolen). Taking the nearby Via della Stella we arrive at the *Oratory of St. Cecilia* of the Philipian Fathers, an important example of Baroque architecture in the round, designed by Pietro Baglioni (1690).

The Church of St. Theresa

On the left, is the **Church of St. Theresa of the Scalzi** (Barefoot). This was the seat of the Barefoot Carmelite sisters up to 1889. Its construction was completed in 1718 to a design by Alessandro Baglioni; the façade is unfinished and the arrangement of the church follows the Greek Cross with a dome in the centre and smaller cupola on the four sides.

Taking Via S. Stefano, we arrive at the **Church of St. Mary of the Francolini**, the façade of which is in Via Francolini. This church already existed in 1166 and was definitely a parish church by 1285; its parish status was transferred to the Church of St. Valentine in 1771; in 1779, it was donated to the 'Servants' of St. Anne. It was renovated in 1580 and rebuilt in 1792 to a design by Alessio Lorenzini. Inside, there are paintings ranging from the 16th to 18th centuries. Above the altar is a canvas by A.M. Garbi which depicts the Virgin, St. Anne and St. Joachine. The famous Perugian judge, Bartolo da Sassoferrato (+ Perugia, 1357) lived in the area of this parish. Further ahead, in Via Vincioli, on the corner with Piazza degli Offici, in the **House of the Missionary Fathers** (now the headquarters of the Finance Office), built in 1755 to a design by Pietro Carattoli.

Proceeding along Via dei Priori, on the left, we come to the famous *Sciri Tower*, the only remaining tower of the numerous ones which must have existed in Perugia. It is 46 metres high and takes its name from the Sciri family — one of the member families of the ruling oligarchy. (In fact, there are other towers still to be seen in Perugia, but they are generally hidden by and incorporated into other buildings). The tower is annexed to a religious institution founded in 1680 by Lucia Tartaglini of Cortona, a Franciscan Tertiary, in order to care for young girls. Today, it is used by the Oblate Sisters and the nuns of St. Philip Neri.

The Church of St. Theresa and the Sciri Tower.

The Oratory of St. Francis

Turning into Via degli Sciri, at no. 6, we find the **Oratory of St. Francis**. The Franciscan brotherhood established itself here in 1319-20. In 1472, it formed a 'confederacy' with the Augustinian and Dominican Brotherhoods: the three orders united with eachother although each retained its own autonomy. The Historical Archives of all three are preserved here (the Braccio Fortebracci Archive). In 1890, they became a Religious Association for mutual aid among the Perugian nobility. These fraternities which had been originally composed of members from different social classes gradually began to restrict their membership to those of noble birth as the gradual process of aristocratic prevalence took hold of Perugia.

The vault of the atrium is decorated with stucco-work by the Frenchman, Jean Regnaud de Champagne (1675-76). In the friars' room, there is a portrait of Braccio Fortebracci (16th century). There is also an architectural relief in wood bearing the names of the Friars (17th century) as well as a 16th-century ballot box. The Oratory is among the most interesting and complete examples of Perugian early-Baroque art and has seats in walnut which were carved by the Perugians, Marco Pace and Sciarra Bovarelli (1584). The prior's seat (1585) and that of the Chairman (1604), are the work of Giampietro Zuccari of Sant'Angelo in Vado who also made the gold-plated frames of several paintings in the Oratory (1618-20). Other frames were made by the Germans, George Rachele of Boeslavia and Stefen Stobe of Regimont (1620). The box ceiling, carved and gold-plated, is the work of Girolamo di Marco, alias the 'Veneziano', and Maestro

Ercole (1570-1574). The altar piece showing the Ascension of Christ is by the Mannerist painter, Leonardo after the style of Michael Angelo (1558). The two works on either side are by the Perugian artist. Paolo Gismondi, a discipline of Pietro da Cortona (1665). On the opposite wall, the paintings of St. Augustine and St. Domenic are by Bernardino Gagliardi (1657). The series of paintings on the theme of Mary and Christ (The Annunciation, Visitation, Nativity, Adoration of the Magi, Presentation in the Temple, Flight into Egypt, the Discussion with the Learned Doctors and the Resurrection) is the most important pictorial ensemble of the Perugian artist, Giovanni Antonio Scaramuccia, painted between 1611 and 1425, except for the Resurrection (1627). In the Sacristy, along with several pieces of liturgical furniture and instruments, is the splendid processional banner of the Brotherhood depicting the Flagellation of Christ by Pietro di Galeotto of Perugia (1480).

1. *Giovanni da Sciampagna: Stucco-work in the atrium (17th century). 2. The Oratory of St. Francis (17th century). 3. The Churches of the Madonna of Light and St. Luke (16th century).*

3

59

At the beginning of the steps of Via del Piscinello, we can observe the **Etruscan Doorway** or **Porta S. Luca** (due to its proximity to the church of St. Luke), sometimes called the Trasimeno doorway as it represents the beginning of the road which leads to Lake Trasimeno and Tuscany. The pointed archway was rebuilt during Mediaeval times.

From here, we can go up the staircase and turn into Via della Sposa; towards the end of this road, on the right, wer come to the **Church of St. Andrew**, already a parish church in 1285; a short way further ahead is the mediaeval **door** of **St. Susanna**. We can continue along the Piaggia Colombata to the **Church of St. Mary of the Colombata** (or Colomata) of which remains the red and white stone façade with its charming gothic doorway. Inside, there are traces of 14th-century frescoes. It was the seat of a community of Benedictine nuns from the end of the 1200's onwards; in 1437, it was closed down because of the licentiousness of the nuns; other nuns resided there during the 15th and 16th centuries but, perhaps because of its position outside the town walls, the place never had a stable community.

1

1. The Trasimena or St. Luke's Gate. 2. The Church of St. Francis: Façade.

The Church of St. Francis

At the end of Via S. Francesco, we come to a piazza dominated by the church of St. Francis al Prato at the side of which, on the left, stands the Oratory of St. Bernardino; a short way ahead, on the right, is the small church of St. Matthew in Campo d'Oro.

Franciscan Minors were already present in Perugia, certainly by 1230, residing at first in the *Pástina* locality, a zone opposite the present church and monastery. In 1253, the friars sold this site together with the structures built on it, to the Benedictine nuns of St. Angelo del Renaio (a convent outside Perugia) for the sum of 2,000 lire, in order to invest in a «loco novo beati Francisi de Perusio posito

in Campo de orto» («a new site for the Perugian Franciscans in the Campo d'orto»). The place which they left and to which the nuns moved, took on the title of St. Francis of the Women (see further on). Between 1248 and 1256, the Franciscans succeeded in obtaining the area of St. Matthew in Campo d'Orto which had belonged to the Monastery of Santa Croce of Fonte Avallana. From this time on, the Minors had a stable community; they built the aisleless church with a transept and polygon-shaped apse. This new church attracted a large congregating many of whom often chose to be buried there or to leave money to the friars. Among those buried there, are the Judge, Bartolo da Sassoferrato and the Mercenary, Braccio Fortebracci. Various aristocratic families aspired to built here their private chapels and sepulchral monuments. With the division of the Franciscan Order into Conventuals and Observants, St. Francis al Prato became (and is still) the seat of the Conventuals while the Observants moved to Monteripido (St. Francis of the Mount).

The church is no longer consecrated and has undergone radical transformations — particularly inside — due to numerous efforts throughout the centuries to prevent the ruination of the walls which stand on unstable terrain. As early as the 1400's, Braccio Fortebracci had consulted architects from Perugia, Siena, Arezzo and even France about the possibility of re-enforcing the church. In the 18th century, another attempt was made under the supervision of Pietro Carattoli (1740 circa). Next to the Oratory of St. Bernardino, is the entrance to the **Academy of Fine Arts**, named after Pietro Vannucci; this, together with the State Institute of Art, occupies the rooms of the former monastery of St. Francis. In the second cloister (the first, designed by Pietro Carattoli has been demolished) there are still

visible some lunettes painted by early-17th century artists from Assisi.

The Academy of Fine Arts, founded in 1573 by Orazio Alfani and Domenico Sozi, established itself in the monastery of St. Francis al Prato towards the beginning of this century. Previously, it hade resided in the Church of St. Angelo della Pace, near porta Sole, and in the convent of Monte Morcino Nuovo. Its important art collection comprises a rich collection of plaster casts (about 500) including a group by Antonio Canova representing the Three Graces (1822), a plaster replica of the one made for the duke of Bedford; the Shepherd by Thorswalden (1832); the four casts after the style of Michael Angelo representing Dawn, Twilight, Day and Night, copied from the originals by Vin-

cenzo Danti (or, as some say, by Michael Angelo himself); there is a collection of paintings, mainly by 19th-century Perugian artists (Gaspare, Sensi, Giuseppe Rossi, Napoleone Verga, Guglielmo Mangiarelli, Matteo Tassi, Mariano Guardabassi, Domenico Bruschi, Annibale Brugnoli, etc.); and a conspicuous selection of drawings and engravings ranging from the 16th to 19th centuries.

The Oratory of St. Bernardino

St. Bernardino of Siena preached in Perugia in 1425, 1438 and 1441; in 1444, he passed through the city but probably did not preach owing to his declining healt. His much-felt impression on Perugian life is apparent in the reform of its statutes (*Statuta Bernardiana*) and in the wide-spread devotion to the name of Jesus, as demonstrated in the name of Jesus, as demonstrated in

1. The Academy of Fine Arts: plaster casts collection. 2. The Academy of Fine Arts: the Museum of the «Ottocento», Domenico Bruschi, a Sketch (19th century).

the trigram IHS, engraved above numerous doorways. Immediately after his canonisation (1450), in 1451, the priors of Perugia decided to honour his memory by building a chapel; thus, the **Oratory of St. Bernardino** was constructed, so admired today for its façade attributed to the Florentine, Agostino di Antonio di Duccio (1457 to 1461). Two lateral pilasters sustain a tympanum and outline the median area which has a twin door above which is a huge lunette. On the tympanum, is a sculpture of Christ among the angels. The words *'Augusta Perusia MCCCCLXI'* are inscribed on the cornice. In the upper niches, on the left, is a statue of Archangel Gabriel and, beneath, there is a bas-relief depicting the Saint welcoming Giacomo della Marca to the Franciscan Order; on the right, is an Annunciation beneath which there is a bas-relief showing the miracle of the star which appeared above the head of the Saint when

he was preaching in Aquila; the lower niches contain statues of St. Costanzo and St. Herculanus (the two patron Bishops of the city) together with St. Lawrence. Beneath them, there is a griffin, the emblem of Perugia. The lunette shows St. Bernardino ascending into the sky amidst angel musicians and cherubs. Below this, divided into three sections, is a panel showing three episodes from the life of the Saint: on the right, a miracle which occurred in Aquila shortly after the death of the Saint; in the centre, we see St. Bernardino preaching to the people of Perugia; on the left, two children are saved form drowing by intercession of the Saint. Below these scenes, is the inscription — «*Opus Augustini Florentini lapicidae*». On the innersides of the doorway, the six Virtues are represented (Religion, Mortification, Pentience, Mercy, Devotion and Purity); towards the exterior are six groups of angel musicians. The interior of the Orato-

1. The Square of St. Francis al Prato. 2. Agostino di Duccio, details of St. Bernardino Oratory façade: the Glory of St. Bernardino. 3. Musician Angels (15th century).

ry is Gothic is form: three sections with a cross-vault. On the right-hand wall there is a copy of the Deposition by Raffaello Baglioni, painted by Orazio Alfani (17th century). The altar is a paleo-Christian tomb in which the body of the Blessed Egidio was placed in 1494. In type, it conforms to the 'columned' sarcophagus style in so far as the front of the cask is divided by columns into niches. In the central niche is the figure of Christ sitting on a throne; on the left, there is a female figure holding a *scroll*; on the right, there is an old beaded man also holding a *scroll*. Beginning from the left, the first niche contains an old man perhaps in the act of preaching, the second contains a young man reading a *croll*. From the right, the first niche has an old man with a *croll* at his feet; in the second, there is the figure of a young man with a rolled up *croll* at his feet. The meaning of this tomb front is by no means clear. On either side of the lid, there

are two male figures (St. Peter? St. Paul?). Left of the *dedicatory tablet* is the figure of Noah waiting to receive the dove and Jonah, thrown out of the belly of the whale; on the right is the scene of Jonah being thrown into the sea. The scenes from the story of Jonah could symbolise the Christian hope of Resurrection. The sarcophagus is attributed to the workshop of Giunio Basso (late 14th century).

Next to the Oratory of St. Bernardino is the **Oratory of SS. Andrew and Bernardino**, also called the Oratory of Justice. The Brotherhood of St. Andrew was formed in 1374 and first resided in the little church of St. Mustiola, a dependent of the Canons of the Church of St. Mustiola in Chiusi. On of the chief functions of the Brotherhood was to give spiritual aid to those condemned to death from which it took on the name of the Brotherhood of Justice. In 1537, it merged with the Brotherhood of St. Bernardino, founded between 1456 and 1460. In the same year, the Brotherhood was given the site near the Church of St. Maria dell'Oliveto, near porta St. Pietro. After this, the present Oratory was built.

We enter the church through a small atrium. On the walls, from right to left, there is a Sermon of St. John the Bap-

tist painted by Marcello Leopardi (1787), a Miracle of St. Bernardino by Carlo Labruzzi (1787) and St. Andrew threatened with floggin by Marcello Leopardi (1785). The later was carved in 1629 and goldplated by Giacomo Agretti in 1762. On the right, there is a canvas depicting the Baptism of Jesus also by Leopardi (1781). The altar is host to a canvas by Gaetano Lapis (1762) depicting the Virgin and Child with St. John the Baptist, St. Andrew and St. Bernardino. Left of the altar is a painting by Marcello Leopardo representing the Decapitation of St. John the Baptist, again by Leopardi (1783). The inner-façade wall has, on the right, a painting of St. Andrew embracing the Cross of his Martyrdom by Vincenzo Ferreri (1790); on the left, St. Bernardino refuses to become a Cardinal, also by Ferreri (1790). The multicoloured marble floor and the walnut pews were made between 1817 and 1818. The box-vaulted ceiling was gold-plated and carved in 1588.

Next to the Church of St. Francis, on the right, is the **Church of St. Mat-**

---

1. The Tomb of Blessed Egidio (15th century). 2. Oratory of Ss. Bernardino and Andrew or of Justice.

thew in Campo d'Orto with its trapezoidal belltower which was transferred here from the demolished Church of St. Mary of Verzaro. This church was the property of the Monastery of S. Croce at Fonte Avellana until its definite concession to the Franciscan Minors (1256). In front of the Church of St. Francis, we observe the fine arch by Valentino Martelli wich was originally located infront of the entrance of the Old University (in Piazza Matteotti).

From the Church of St. Francis, we proceed along Via Alessandro Pascoli. We can deviate into Via dell'Eremita, reaching as far as the small piazza in which the **Church of SS. Sebastian and Rocco** is situated. This church took on parochial status when the Church of St. Elizabeth was demolished.

This area of the city is known as the «Conca» (basin) on account of its position between the elevated areas of Verzato and porta St. Angelo.

Around the beginning of the 13th century this area, which belonged to the Chathedral, began to become populated, taking on the characteristics of a 'borgo' (quarter) whilst maintaining its surrounding fields and orchards. Thus, we have another example of mediaeval urban expansion: in fact, where the ends of Via Goldoni and Via del Maneggio meet, we find the old Conca Gateway, built entirely in travertine rock; at the end of Via A. Pascoli, we find the 'new' Conca Gateway with its mediaeval wall, erected during the first half of the 14th century.

A pre-existing chapel had been given to the Brotherhood of St. Sebastian in 1484; in the early 1500's, after a miraculous event attributed to the image of the Madonna of the Mild (15th century), which can still be inside, the small church was enlarged and took on the name of Madonna della Pace (of Peace). From the mid-1600's on, a community of her-

mits resided behind the oratory; amongst these Francesco Van-Outers from Brussels who died in 1729.

The internal walls have frescoes by Pietro Montanini representing episodes from the lives of SS. Sebastian and Rocco, scenes from the Day of Judgement and pictures of St. John in the Desert and St. Onofrio (1665 circa). The paintings on the box ceiling and in the Presbytery (beyond the wrought iron grille) are the work of Giovan Francesco Bassoti (1665). In the right-hand chapel there is a canvas showing scenes from the life of St. Onofrio attributed to Pietro Montanini (1672), taken from the Dyers' altar in the nearby Church of St. Elizabeth.

From Via dell'Eremita, taking Via St. Sebastian, we arrive in Via S. Elisabetta, infront of the Faculty of Chemistry. Here, beyond the outer walls of the now demolished parish Church of St. Elizabeth (1337 circa), there is a large mosaic dating back to the 11th century, possibly part of a thermal complex, which depicts Orpheus persued by the furies.

On reaching the Conca Gateway at the end of Via A. Pascoli, we turn into Via St. Galgano. On the left, we see the Dyers' Fountain, erected, in 1388. The dyers' trade was one of the most widespread among the inhabitants of the Conca. Taking the communal road of S. Lucia, still on the left, we reach the arcient **fountains of St. Galgano**. In 1279, a Benedictine convent was already established here. In 1412, it merged with the convent of St. Francis of the Women. The area possessed natural springs which were thought to have hearling powers. In 1635-40, a thermal bath was built here. After the Unification, in 1862, a company was formed to exploit the potential of the said springs. From the beginning of the 1900's the spring of St. Galgano began to fall into desuse. Continuing along this road, we ascend the hill of **Monte Morcino Vecchio** where, in 1366, in accordance with the wishes of Cardinal Nicolò Capocci, a community of Olivetans was founded which destined to remain there until 1749, when the construction of the 'New' Monastery of Monte Morcino was begun. A few 14th-century remnants of the monastic buildings are still visible. They are thought to be the work of Francesco di Guido of Settignano.

Continuing along Via F. Innamorati ant then a stretch of Via Z. Faina, we reach the **former Monastery of St. Francis of the Women** which was probably Perugia's first Franciscan community; it was taken over by the Benedictine nuns of Angelo del Renaio (see further back - St. Francis al Prato), who remained here up to 1815, the year in which the convent was suppressed; it was then converted to secular use.

On the return journey from the Conca, we can reach the town centre by climbing the steps of Via Appia. Of particular note are the arches — restored in 1516 by Vincenzo Danti — of the aqueduct which was built during the second half of the 13th centu-

1. A Roman Mosaic (200 A.D.). 2. The Church of Monte Morcino Nuovo (18th century).

68

2

ry, trasporting water from Monte Pacciano to the famous fountain.

Almost at the end of Via Appia, we can see the Etruscan Arch of which only a few gothic remains are left.

Here, we find ourselves in Via Baldeschi and directly on our left is Piazza Cavallotti with its 16th-century Palazzo Baldeschi.

From Piazza Cavallotti, we can turn into the characteristic Via del Verzaro. At he beginning, no. 3, closed in between the buildings, is a typical mediaeval tower. A few yeards ahead we come to the **Church of St. Martin of Verzaro**, today an Encumenical Centre; this building dates back to before 1163; it was partly dependent on the Canons of the Cathedral and partly on the Monastery of St. Angelo of Chiaserra (Diocese of Gubbio). In 1257, the Abbot of St. Angelo turned his part over to the Monastery of St. Juliana in Perugia. In 1285, it became a parish church and continued to belong to the Cathedral Charter until the end of the 1500's. It is an aisleless church with a small trapezoidal bell-tower. Inside, on the wall behind the altar, there are frescoes attributed to Gianni-cola di Paolo (Virgin and Child, St. Lawrence and St. John): the right-hand section of the far wall depicts the scene in which St. Martin gives half his cloak to a beggar, by a Perugian artist; the left-hand section shows the Crucifixion with Mary Magdalen, Our Lady and St. John by a Mannerist artist.

Going back down Via del Verzaro, still on the right, is Piazza Morlacchi, dominated by an attractive 18th-century building, today the seat of the Faculty of Letters; next to this is the **Communal Francesco Morlacchi Theatre**, built in 1778-80 on the innitiative of the new up-and-coming bourgeoisie who wished to emulate the nobility which had financed the construction of the Pavone Theatre (see further on). The architect was the Perugian, Alessio Lorenzini; the theatre was restored in 1874 and was dedicated to Perugia's most famous musician. Opposite the theatre is the Palazzo Bianchi, begun in 1873 and built to a design by Gugliel-mo Calderini; it is a good example of Perugian bourgeois architecture.

The Maestà delle Volte (Her Majesty of the Vaults)

From Piazza Cavallotti, we return

2

to Piazza Grande taking the Via Maestà delle Volte. This was the dark Mediaeval thoroughfare in which the votive image of the Virgin and Child was painted in 1297. In front of this image a lamp shone continuously. After a while, in recognition of the devotion of the people, a church was built; among those who worked on the façade, was Agostino di Antonio di Duccio (some of his sculptures are exhibited in the Umbrian National Gallery). The area suffered extensive damage during a fire in 1534. In 1566, the 'jus patronatus' of the church passed from the city to the seminary. Between 1580 and 1590, the church took on its present form which was based on a plan by Bino Sozi. The church has now been converted into a shop for religious

1

1. Via Appia. 2. The Church of St. Martino del Verzaro: Giannicola di Paolo (?), Madonna and Child with Saints (16th century). 3. Via Maestà delle Volte. 4. Maestà delle Volte, mediaeval archway.

ornaments. However, it still contains ancient frescoes (much-repainted) whose unknown author is traditionally referred to as the 'Maestro della Maestà delle Volte'. The frescoes in the vault are signed by Nicolò Circignani, the so-called 'Pomarancio' (1568). On the left is a fine arch, built in red and white marble; it is probably a remnant of a 14th-century portico; on the right is a modern work depicting the Virgin of testà delle Volte by G. Belletti (1945). The fountain in a hollow beneath the church is by the architect, Pietro Angelini (1929).

From Piazza Matteotti we turn into Via Oberdan. Part of this road was occupied by by the **Hospice of St. Mary of Mercy** (della Misericordia) and its connected church. Its engraved emblem is still visible at nos. 40 and 58 (a trigram consisting of the uncial letters d, m, e = domus Misericordie).

In 1296, the Brotherhood of Mercy had already existed for sometime, composed of clerics and laymen; however, it was in 1305 that the Bishop of Perugia officially recognised the foundation of the Hospice of St. Mary of Mercy to accomodate pilgrims, the poor and infirm and abandoned chil-

4

dren. From this time on, it developed into the most important charity and welfare institution in the city. From 1862, it was run by the Perugian Congregation of Charity. At no. 54, we can see the door of the church which was renovated in 1760 to a design by Pietro Carattoli. On the left, there is a large niche containing a figure of Our Lady of Mercy attributed to Giovan Battista Caporali (16th century); on the right, a small niche contains a Madonna between two angels attributed to Martino da Perugia (14th century).

Descending the St. Herculanus staircase, before reaching the church, we come across a gate called the **arch of St. Herculanus** (or the Cornea or Berarda Arch), the lower area of which is Etruscan while the arch is decidely Gothic.

3

4 Itinerary

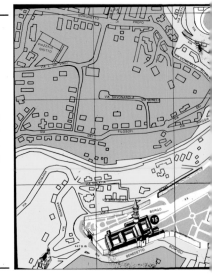

The Church or St. Herculanus - The Church of St. Dominic - The Archaeological Museum - Porta S. Pietro - The Church of St. Peter - The Rocca Paolina.

The Church or St. Herculanus

The **Church of St. Herculanus** — the 'defensor civitas' Bishop, symbol of the city's municipal autonomy — was built during the first decades of the 14th century. It had the form of a polygon shaped tower and was originally composed of two separate levels. The upper level (with its entrance in the present-day Via Marzia) was destroyed after the construction of the Rocca Paolina in order to afford a better view of the valley. In 1607, Bishop Napoleon Comitoli sponsored a renovation of the building which had already begun in 1604, with the construction of the double-flighted staircase replacing the old semi-circular one built out of the stones taken from the 13th-century Arnolfo Fountain. Inside, the cupola and lunettes are painted with scenes from the life of St. Paul by Giovanni Andrea Carlone from Genoa (1675). The monochrome gold-finished decorations are by Nicola Giuli. On the right, is the Chapel of St. Charles Borromeo containing stucco-work (1682) by the Frenchman, Jean Regnaud (Giovanni di Sciampagna) who also did the

stucco-work in the opposite Chapel of St. Martin. The altar-piece of this Chapel shows a Miracle worked by St. Martin and is attributed to Anton Maria Garbi. The central area of the apse is occupied by a copy of Pietro Perugino's Decemvir altar-piece, perhaps by Biagio di Angelo. On each side there is a painting by Giovanni Andrea Carlone (St. Peter and St. Paul) and two paintings (four in all) by Mattia Salvucci showing episodes from the life of St. Herculanus (1627 circa). The main altar is composed of a fine 4th-century sarcophagus, discovered in 1609 in the Church of St. Orfito near depict-

The Gardens and Church of St. Herculanus.

ty to the great Abbey of St. Peter and the Church of St. Costanzo; it was also the beginning of the road leading to Assisi and Rome. On the right, on the corner with Via Marconi, we see the ancient **Church of S. Croce** which used to belong to the Knights of the Holy Sepulchre from the late 1100's. Towards the ent. of the 19th century, it was taken over by Company of St. Joseph of the Carpenters, founded in 1577 by a master carpenter. It thus takes its present neme of St. Joseph's from this company. Its interior contains an unattached much-repainted eraly 15th-century fresco, depicting Our Lady of Mercy. On the left, there is a canvas showing Our Lady between SS. Joseph and Claud by Giovanni Antonio Scaramuccia (1632 circa); on the right is another canvas emulating the style of Ludovico Carracci, possibly by Luigi Scaramuccia (17th century).

ing Mary as a Child, St. Anne and St. Joachine by Anton Maria Garbi (18th century).

At the end of the staircase of St. Herculanus, we turn left into Corso Cavour. This was one of the main street which linked the old ci-

The Church of St. Dominic

From here, we proceed ahead until we reach Piazza Giordano Bruno which is dominated by the imposing structure of the **Church of St. Dominic**. Of interest is the piazza's fine well-curb dating. 1452. During the early Middle Ages, this area was the site of the local horse market and fair.

The Dominican Order was admitted to this area in 1234, at which time it was still part of the parish of St. Stephen of Castellare, listed in the Cathedral Charter sometime before 1163. In 1304, the parish was definitively conceded to the Preaching friars by Benedict XI in order to extend the Church of St. Dominic. The same Pope later granted a plenary indulgence to this church for having claimed to contain the body of St. Stephen the Martyr, obviously in competition with the Porziuncola in Assisi. After 1437, the Monastery of St. Dominic passed into the hands of the Observants; it became the seat of a *Studium* and, during the 1400's was elevated to the rank of '*Studium solemne*'.

Tradition has it that the church was designed by Giovanni Pisano. In any case, its construction was completed in 1458, the year in which it was consecrated to St. Stephen by Pope Pius II. Before the 17th-century renovation of the interior (by Carlo Maderno - 1632), the building presented an enormous 'hallenkirche' plan with octogonal pilasters in laterite stone, pointed arches and large stained-glass windows. The bell-tower was once surmonted by a high steeple dating from the late 1400's and was the work or Gasperino di Antonio of

Lombardy. It was shortened during the 15th century, probably for reasons of instability, although tradition identifies in this act the same motivations which prompte Pope Paul III to demolish the upper level of the church of St. Herculanus. The front staircase was designed by Girolamo Ciofi of Cortona (1640). The doorway is dated 1596. Above it remain traces of a rose-window by Benedetto di Valdorcia of Siena (1415).

Following this, there is the former Chapel of St. Peter the Martyr, transformed during the 18th century into a side entrance to the church. In a niche on the right-hand wall, we find the sepulchral monument of Judge Guglielmo Pontano after the style of Sansovini (16th century). The south transept (at the head of which the Chapel of St. Domenic was built in 1450, similar to the Banner Chapel in St. Francis al Prato) contains two 18th-century canvases. The Chapel of St. Peter the Martyr (first on the right of the four chapels in the apse) contains a painting by Bonaventura Borghesi of Cortona (1705) depicting the Martyrdom of St. Peter together with remains of votive frescoes from the 14th and 15th centuries. Next to this, is the Chapel of the Apostles (now or Blessed Benedict XI) with vault

1. The Church of St. Domenic. 2. The Church of St. Domenic: Interior.

frescoes depcting the various Dominican saints by a late-gothic artist of the early 15th century. on the right-hand wall, is the sepulchral monument of Benedict XI (14th century) transferred here from the Church of St. Domenic during the 18th century. Structurally speaking, it resembles the form of the sepulchtral monument of Cardinal Guglielmo De Braye by Arnolfo di Cambio in the Church of St. Domenic in Orvieto (1282 circa) and it is traditionally thought to be work of Vasary and Giovanni Pisano. However, its stylistic similarities with the Cathedral of Orvieto leads to the conclusion that, in fact, it is the work of an Umbrian artist of the Tuscan school. The monument consists of a shrine resting upon twisting columns with marble tarsia-work and cherubs underwhich there is a canopy and the reposing figure of the deceased; the sarcophagus is surmonted by a plaque with figures of saints and a millioned-window with three lights showing the Virgin, St. Domenic and the kneeling Pope. On the column separating this chapel from the apse, there is the tomb of Elizabeth Cantucci de Colis with a valuable bust by Alessandro Algardi (1648); on the opposite column is the sepulchral monument of the prelate Alessandro Benincasa with a marble bust by Domenico Guidi (1594). The main altar, begun in 1720 to a design by Pietro Carattoli, was completed in a successive epoch and in a style not entirely in keeping with the original plan. The apse remained completely unaffected by the 17th-century renovation works and has a large Renaissance Choir begun in 1476 by Crispolito da Bettona (the section on the left) with the help of Polimante della Spina and Giovanni Schiavo (the section on the right). The marquetry-work is by Antonio da Mercatello (1498). At the centre, there is a huge ogival window — one of the largest in Italy after the

ones in Milan Cathedral — with stained-glass made in 1411 by the Perugian, Bartolomeo di Pietro and Mariotto di Nardi, a Florentine. The left-hand pillaster of the Presbytery is host to the sepulchral monument of the Danti family with a bush of Vincenzio, sculpted by Valerio Cioli (16th century). The next chapel (previously of St. Nicholas, now the Chapel of the Name of Jesus) has a painting of the Circumcision by Giuseppe Berettini (17th century), nephew and disciple of Pietro da Cortona. On the left, is the sepulchral monument of

Bishop Benedetto Guidalotti (1429) attributed to Urban of Cortona. In 1437, to honour this family and its chapel, Beato Angelico painted a beautiful polyptych now preserved in the Umbrian National Gallery. The right-hand wall shows St. Ursula and the Virgins by Benedetto Bandiera (17th century). The four section of the vault bear frescoes by a Giottesque artist, recently identified as Allegretto Nuzi from the Marches region (14th century).

The Sacristy is a large square-shaped ambient, built in the 14th century and modified in the 1700's. The centre of the vault and the lunettes bear frescoes by Mattia Battini. Along the walls are portraits of Popes and Cardinals of the Domenican Order; it also contains numerous pieces of 18th-century furniture. A 17th-century canvas by Benedetto Bandiera hangs above the altar. A showcase built into the wall contains belongings of Benedict XI (dalmatic, surplice, boots, sceptre, stole and slippers) all articles dating from the 14th century.

Going back into the Church, the first chapel in the north aisle (the Chapel of St. Catherine), still in the

1. The Sepulchral Monument of Benedict XI (14th century). 2. Alessandro Algardi: the Bust of Elisabetta Cantucci (17th century).

Gothic style, contains numerous rather fragmented frescoes, said to be the work of Varsari di Taddeo di Bartolo but more probably that of Benedetto di Bindo and his pupils (1415 circa). There follows: the Chapel of the Resurrection or Rosary which has above the altar a painting of the Madonna and Child together with SS. Domenic and Catherine of Siena by Giovanni Lanfranco (1647); the Banner Chapel, named after the Banner by Giannicola di Paolo (1494), contained therein, depicting, in the upper section Christ, with the Virgin Mary, St. John and other saints, whilst the lower section depicts a group of faithful between St. Domenic and the Blessed Colomba, an interesting example of Perugian art of this period; the Chapel of St. Vincent Ferreri, containing a canvas (1730) by Francesco Busti and another representing St. Luke (1675 circa) by Giovanni Andrea Carlone; the Chapel of Our Lady of Sorrows with a wooden Pietà dating from the 17th century after the style of Micheal Angelo.

At no. 6, Piazza Giordano Bruno, we see the entrance to the **cloister** of the monastery, one of the largest in the city with fourty travertine columns. It was begun in 1455 and finished in 1589. One side of the cloister incorporates the façade of the old gothic Church of St. Dominic with its twin portal in white and red stone. Beside this, is a gate leading into another cloister which contains the entrance to the **Perugian State Archives**, one of the richest in Italy; it possesses important historical sources regarding the city, amongst them — *The Historical Archive of the Perugia Commune* and the *Suppressed Religious Associations*, as well as a cospicuous collection of notarial documents.

The Archaeological Museum

The arcade is the home of the **Archaeological Museum**.

The Museum has its origins in a donation made by Francesco Filippo Friggeri who gave his valuable collection of Etruscan and Roman works to the city of Perugia in 1790. This collection was subsequently added to by donations from the following families: Oddi, Graziani, Ansidei, Guardabassi, Bellucci (amulets) and Antinori (African objects). After a brief spell in the Priors' Palace, the Museum was transferred to the Monastery of Monte Morcino Nuovo in 1812; in 1936, it was moved again to Palazzo Donini-Ferretti where it remained until 1948 when it was finally settled in its present location (the former Monastery of St. Dominic). Here, it took on the status of Communal Civic Museum in 1962.

The Museum occupies part of the large Cloister and the second floor fo the Monastery. In the Cloister,

below the portico, Etruscan cinerary urns, inscriptions and architectural fragments are on display. Of particular interest are the following: a black and white mosaic with geometrical motifs dating back to 100 B.C. from the Perugia area; a sarcophagus showing the myth of Meleagrus (late 1000's A.D.) from Farfa; a well-curb depicting a battle between Greeks and Amasons, also from Farfa; several Augustan memorial stones with the inscription 'Perusia restituta'. Not far from the staircase leading up to the second floor, there is a Roman plaque with decorative motifs, used as an altar table during the Middle Ages.

In the gallery of the second floor, numerous Etruscan urns are displayed, originating from various Perugian necropolis (400-100 B.C.),

1. The Cloister of St. Domenic's: Remnants of the façade of St. Domenico Vecchio. 2. Cola Petruccioli(?): the Martyrdom of St. Peter (14th century).

put into categories according to their place of origin. The southern section displays urns from the ten necropolis around Ponticello di Campo; the western gallery contains urns originating from the families Rafia (of Perugia), Pomponia and Plotia (the Hypogeum of the Volumni), Noforsinia (from the necropolis of the Palazzone), Titia Vetia (from San Sisto) and various others from the Monteluce area. At the centre of this gallery, there is a Perugian urn in terracotta (300 B.C.) showing the reclining figure of the deceased on the lid and the legend of the monster coming out of the well on the front. The northern vallery contains urns of various origins, including those of the following families: Trebia (from Castiglione del Lago), Tetinia (from Paciano) and Varna (from Cetona). The eastern gallery contains Roman remains, cinerary urns and inscriptions. Several inscriptions originate from Arna.

The corridor leading to the gallery of the second cloister contains several Roman portraits including a head of Claudius discovered at Carsulae; a portrait of Caesar, one of Augustua and one of a woman with a hair-style like that of Agrippina, from Carsulae and Spoleto respectively. At the end of the corridor there are two different sections: Prehistoric on the left, Etruscan/Roman on the right.

The Prehistoric section occupies eight rooms, a long corridor and a large hall; the material is displayed according to typology and the place of origin. The rooms containing works ordered according to object type (four on the right and one on the left of the corridor) display palaeolithic and neolithic material from the Bellucci Collection originating from Umbria, Tuscany, the Marches and Abruzzo. In the last three rooms, the material is arranged topographically and originates from the various prehistoric settlements existing in the region of Perugia. Leaving the corridor, a staircase leads up to the hall containing material from the Bronze

2

and Iron Ages. Part of the Hall is occupied by material from Monte Cetona (the Calzoni excavation), dating from the middle palaeolithic age (the Gosto Grotta); and material from the Bronze age (the Carletti house).

Descending the staircase we enter the Etruscan/Roman section, at present in the process of being re-ordered. ROOM I contains a grave stele found at Monte Gualandro, originating from Tuoro, showing battle scenes (early 4th century B.C.). The corridor contains a sepulchral sphinx from the Cetona area (late 6th century).

ROOM II is host to Chiusian memorial stone with relief and poly-chromatic work (late 6th and 5th centuries B.C.); backing onto the far wall, is a sandstone sarcophagus from the Sperandio necropolis near Perugia, with relief-work on the front and polychromatic traces on the sides. It depicts a triumphal return from battle with banqueting scenes (late 6th century B.C.). ROOMS III and IV preserve embossed bronze laminas and statues from Castel San Marino near Corciano.

1. Western arm of the loister of St. Domeniċ's: Etruscan Urns. 2. Cinerary Urn. 3. Perugian stone. 4. Sandstone sarchophagus (from the Sperandio area). 5. Bronze dagger (from Fontivegge).

The bronze laminas (some of which are on display in the British Museum) are among the rarest of the archaic bronze-work to be found in the Etruscan territories. They probably constituted the covering of a war chariot.

ROOM V contains objects from the necropolis of Monteluce whilst ROOM VI is nost to material discovered in the necropolis of Frontone: of particular importance is a make funeral 'corredo' including arms, bronze kottabos and attic vase with red figures from the. myth of Trittolemo and a bronze lid. ROOM VII has objects from the necropolis of Santa Caterina and Sperandio; from the first, among other interesting objects, there is a bronze situla with a siren on the lid and a gold earing (the other of which is in the British Museum). Outside ROOM VII is the famous Perugian Memorial Stone in travertine rock with one of the longest Etruscan inscriptions yet to be discovered mentioning the Velthina and Afuna families, properties and tombs. ROOM VIII accomodates material from the Perugian necropolis of Santa Giuliana, Ponticello di Campo, Monte Vile, Cimitero. ROOM IX con-

3

Sarcofago in arenaria (dallo Sperandio)

4

tains objects from the sepulchres in the immediate vicinity of the city (Monte Tezio, Pila, Bettona). ROOM X displays material from Orvieto and around Castiglione del Lago: of particular interest is a Greek helmet with decorative motifs in relief and several urns from Paciano. ROOM XI is host to votive objects from Colle Arsiccio (terracotta statues) and Caligiano di Magione as well as votive bronzes from the sanctuaries of Ancarano di Norcia and Calvi. In the corridor, we find a terracotta statue of Hercules, signed by the artist (C. Rufius s(igillator) finxit), from Compresso.

To the right of the corridor is the entrance of the 17th-century gallery in which Cypriot material (16th to 1st century B.C.) from the Palma di Cesnola collection is on display along with Corinthian and Etrusco-Corinthian ceramics and Attic and Etruscan ceramics with black and red figures. Without doubt, the most valuable object is the Volterrano Kelebe showing the myth of Hercules and Hesion and of Hercules and Ketos attributed to the Hesion artist and dating back to around the late 4th century B.C.

Next to the Church of St. Dominic, we can take Via del Castellano which is bordered on the right by the south aisle chapel walls of the church. The first three are in laterite stone and date from the 18th century. To the left of the site entrance, note the polygon-shaped rock structure of the present Chapel of St. Domenic built by Giovanni and Luchino di Pietro during the 1450's in accordance to the wishes of the Perugian merchant, Francesco di Pietro. The rhythm of the red and white stone work is interrupted by a large gothic mullioned-window; the upper region bears a dentil shaped ornamentation also in red and white stone.

The house next to the *Auditorium Marianum* contains an early 14th-century painting of the Madonna and Child.

Porta S. Pietro (St. Peter's Gate)

Porta S. Pietro is, in fact, composed of two separate gateways. The internal one presents clear traces of successive renovations: the main part is built in ashlar-work travertine and red stone, typical of Perugian and Umbrian mediaeval constructions, and laterite. Above the arch, there is a niche containing figures of Our Lady of the Rosary between SS. Dominic and Francis; the image was painted in 1765 and re-painted in 1817. The external gateway has all the elegance of the Humanist/Renaissance period and is reminiscent of the Malatestian Temple by Alberti in Rimini. It is the work of Agostino di Antonio di Duccio and Polidoro di Stefano of Perugia and was built during the

1. St. Peter's Gate. 2. St. Peter's Gate: detail.

period, 1475-1480. The central arch is decorated by a festoon and the piers show evidence of the fluting of the slide gate. On either side, there are two towers with elegant parastas, surmounted by Corinthian capitals.

On the left, between the two gateways, we find the small travertine Renaissance portal of the **Church of St. James**, an ancient parish church (1285) which contains a painting depicting the Crucifix between SS. James and John the Baptist, signed by Benedetto Bandiera (17th century).

Continuing down Viale Benedetto Bonfigli, we can see on our left, at no. 8, the coat-of-arms of the Exchange: a griffin above a chest; this marks the site of the hospice of this guild. A little further down, on the right, we find the former *Monastery of St. Jerome*. This was the seat of the Amadeam friars from 1483 to 1568, the year of their suppression by Pius V; after this, the brothers dedicated themselves to those stricken by plague; after a time, they merged with the Franciscan Observants and continued to work with them until the supression of the post Unification period. Of this monastery, we can still see and early 18th century portico designed by Pietro Carattoli and the internal cloister with its laterite archways dating from the 17th century. Further down, we find the **Alexandrian Gate** (sometimes called the **Gate of St. Jerome**). It was built towards the end of the 1400's and was reconstructed by order of the delegate Cardinal Alexander Riario in 1582.

The Church of St. Peter

Proceeding along Via Borgo XX Giugno, we arrive at the **Church and Abbey of St. Peter**.

A church has existed in the area — called Monte Cavlario of Capraio — since the times of Pope Gregory the Great. In fact, tradition has it that this was the site of the first Cathedral of Perugia. The monastery is said to have been established around the year 966 A.D., on the initiative. of the Blessed Pietro Vincioli, but, in reality, its origins go further back into obscurity. It is certain that, in the Roman Synod of 1002, Pope Sylvester II decided to defend the Abbot of St. Peter's against the Bishop of Perugia, Canone, who had invaded the monastery, declaring it to be the property of the Roman Church and, therefore, under the jurisdiction of the Bishop. The monastery's archive preserves a large quantity of papal privileges an imperial favours, awarded to the Abbey during the 11th and 12th centuries all evidence of its importance and wealth. Throughout the 13th century, it continued to receive papal protection and, during the reign of Gregory IX, statutes for the reform

2

of the monastery were drawn up (1235?). During the 14th century, the monastery suffered a period of crisis and confusion; in 1398, the Perugians set fire to the monastery when they rose against Abbot Francis Guidalotti who, with his brother, was the author of the conspiracy against Biordo Michelotti, head of the popular party. In 1436, in order to relieve conditions within the monastery, Pope Eugene IV merged it with the Congregation of St. Justina of Padua. Following this union, the monastery refluorished, resuming and maintaining its prestige and power within the town. In 1799, the monastery was suppressed by the French and then restored to the monks by the provisional Austri-

an/Aretine Government. In reward for having assisted several leaders of the Perugian revolt of 1859, after Unification, the monks were allowed to stay on at the Abbey.

Passing through a monumental front section with three arches, designed around 1614 by the Perugian architect, Valentino Martelli, with the explicit intention of corresponding to the opposite 15th-century gateway by Agostino di Duccio, we enter into the first cloister of the monastery, the lower region of which was also designed by Valentino Martelli. The upper floor is attributed to Lorenzo Petrozzi who, after Martelli, was entrusted with the task of completing the works.

In the north cloister, we arrive at

1

the entrance of the Church. On either side of this Quattrocento doorway, surmounted by a lunette and attributed to Giannicola di Paolo, we can see the remains of the ancient façade of the basilica which included a portico of small arches in red and white and 13th and 14th-century frescoes. Right of the doorway, the base of the large polygon shaped bell-towers is still visible: we can still recognise the gothic forms of the Tuscan type which originated from the 15th-century reconstruction, particularly in the bell-tower and spire, attributed to the Florentine, Giovanni di Betto and Pietro di Firenze, working to a design by Bernardo Rossellino (1463-1468).

Its interior with a nave and two aisles, contains the finest art collection in Perugia after the Umbrian National Gallery.

The nave is divided from the aisles by a series of arches, sustained by columns probably originating from ancient Roman buildings. The upper regions are decorated with large canvases depicting scenes from the New and Old Testaments paired with panels according to the theological and didactic contents which are clearly linked to Counter-Reformation doctrine. This scheme presents a unified iconographical programme, including the pictures in the presbytery, which was almost certainly the idea of Abbot Don Giacomo da San Felice of Salò and it was arranged between 1591 and 1611. The canvases are the work of Antonio Vassillacchi, alias the 'Alinese', a disciple of Veronese but, above all, of Tintoretto, and were painted in Venice between 1593 and 1594.

Beginning from the right, they are as follows: the Birth of Jesus and Isaac blessing Jacob; the Dispute with the Doctors and the Queen of Sheba admiring the wisdom of Solomon; the Baptism of Christ and Naaman cured of Leprosy; the Wedding of Cana and the meal given by Abraham to the three angels; Jesus dining with the

1. The Church of St. Peter. 2. Historic façade.

Pharisee and the penitence of David when reproved by the Prophet Natham; the Resurrection of Lazarus and Elias raising from the dead, the son of the widow of Sereptas; the Expulsion of the Merchants from the Temple and Moses breaking the tablets of the commandments; the Entrance of Jesus into Jerusalem and David conquering Goliath, the Crucifixion and the Sacrifice of Isaac; the Resurrection and Jonah surrended by the Whale.

The large canvas depicting the Triumph of the Benedicting Order, on the innerfaçade wall, is also by Antonio Vassillacchi.

The frescoes on the walls are attributed to Giovanni Maria Bisconti whilst the ovals, set within the triangles of the arche showing the busts of various Popes, are the work of Benedetto Bandiera who also painted the Virgin and the Archangel Gabriel on the triumphal arch. The decorations on the vault of the south aisle are probably by Scilla Pecennini and Benedetto

Bandiera; whilst those in the north aisle, unfortunately, much repainted, bear a marked resemblance to the work of Mattia Salvucci of Perugia.

On either side of the outer door, made by Pompeo Dardoni in 1682, there are detached frescoes by Orazio Alfani and Leonardo Cungi from Borgo San Sepolcro (1556). The former painted the ones on the left depicting St. Peter healing the Cripple and St. Peter being freed from the prison; Cungi painted the Shipwreck of St. Paul and St. Paul landing in Malta. The ceiling of the nave, with carved and gold-plated box vaulting, is the work of Benedetto di Giovanni Pierantonio of Montepulciano (1564).

Beginning our tour of the church from the south aisle, the first work we meet is a Virgin and Child between SS. Mary Magdalen and George by Eusebio da San Giovanni

Interior.

(16th century). There follows a panel depicting the Assumption of Mary with the Apostles, by Orazio Alfani (16th century). The canvas above the following altar showing St. Scolastica is by Francesco Appiani (1751). Further on, we find a canvas by the Classical artist, Giacinto Gimignani with St. Peter stopping a falling column with a sign of the cross (1679). The second altar has a canvas by Cesare Sermei of Assisi depicting St. Marius resurrecting a man from the dead. The following painting of David choosing among the three punishments threatened by the angel, is by the Sienese baroque artist, Ventura Salimbeni (1602). The hanging canvas above the third altar shows the Procession of Penitence made in Rome by St. Gregory the Great together with the people at the time of the Great Plague. It also includes a panel attributed to Eusebio da San Giorgio who was author of the predella depicting scenes from the life of St. Christine (16th century). A little futher ahead, we arrive at the chapel of St. Joseph, commissioned in 1855 by the Abbot, Placido Acquacotta. It was painted by the Perugian artist Domenico Bruschi, assisted by Giovanni Panti. The altar painting which was recently stolen was a copy of a Raphael by Carlo Fantacchiotti (19th century). The entrance is surmounted by a lunette in the Perugian style depicting Our Lady, the Holy Child and four Saints (16th century); the panel on the right-hand wall of the Virgin and Child and SS. John and Elizabeth (16th century) is of the Tuscan school. Going back into the nave, we immediately come across a painting by the French artist, Francios Perrier depicting Samson destroying the columns of the temple (17th century). Opposite, there is a fine Pietà of the school of Sebastiano del Piombo (16Th century). Following this, is the door leading into the monastery, above which are three square panels: the central one, of the Venetian school resembles the style of Bonifacio da Verona; the lateral ones, depicting St. Placido and St. Marius are copied from Perugino by Giovan Battista Salvi, alias 'Sassoferrato' (17th century). Opposite, is a Virgin and Child by the Perugian classicist, Giovan Domenico Cerrini (17th century). This artist also painted the St. John the Baptist above the gap leading into the Presbystery area. Just before the Sacristy door, there is a Resurrection of Christ by Orazio Alfani (1553).

Above the door, there are three square panels depicting St. Flavia, St. Apollonia and St. Catherine of Sassoferrato (the last two of which are copies of works by Perugino). The far end of the aisle is host to the Chapel of the Relics or of the Angels with a 16th-century wrought-iron grille, late 16th-century stucco work and rather damaged frescoes by Benedetto Bandiera (1602 circa). This artist also painted the altar-piece depicting St. Benedict in Glory among the angels, at present to be seen in the Great Hall of the Faculty of Agriculture.

The Sacristy (1451) has a vault bearing frescoes with stories from the Old Testament framed by decorative motifs traditionally attributed to the Perugian artist, Scilla Pecennini. However, it is more probable that they are the work of an artist connected with the Nordic and Flemish presence documented in Perugia during the 1560's. The wall frescoes depicting the lives of SS. Peter and Paul are by Girolamo Danti (1574), an artist of Varsarian formation. The majolica floor, traces of which are visible in front of the altar, is a splendid work by Giacomo Mantini (El frate) and dates back to 1563-64. The wardrobes were made by Giusto di Francesco di Incisa and

Giovanni di Filippo da Fiesole (1472). On the altar, by Guido di Virio of Settignano and also decorated with paintings by Girolamo Danti, there is a bronze Crucifix by Algardi (17th century). There are numerous small paintings on the wall including a series of Saints by Perugino (St. Costanzo, St. Peter Abbot, St. Herculanus and St. Scolastica - a copy of the original) which together with others belong to the altar-piece of the Ascension today in the Museum of Lyon (1496); a panel with two cherubs by an imitator of Perugino, inspired by the Holy Family in the Museum of Marseille; two canvases in the style of Caravaggio (St. Frances Romana and Christ with the Crown of Thorns); a head of Christ resembling the style of Dosso

Dossi; a 16th-century Holy Family of the Emilian school and a Visitatio by a disciple of Sebastiano Conca.

Going back into the aisle, we find ourselves in the area of the Presbytery. The two polygon-shaped stone pulpits are the work of Francesco da Guido of Settignano, made between 1487 and 1530; the seat has a wealth of gold-plated carvings by Benedetto da Montepulciano and Benvenuto da Brescia (1555-56). Of the two organs, the one nearer the Sacristy was almost completely remade in 1591. The lower part is decorated with allegorical figures attributed to Benedetto Bandiera but was carried out with the help of an unknown baroque artist of great stylistic elegance. The other organ is the work

The inner front of the triumphal arch is decorated with harvesting and reaping scenes taken from the Apocalypse and attributed to Giovanni Fiammingo of Anvers (1592). The vault between the presbytery and chior (God the Father among the Angels) and the lunettes between the ribbing of the apse (The Theological and Cardinal Virtues) are painted by Scilla Pecennini with the collaboration of Pietro d'Alessandro (1594). Finally, we come across the two famous scenes of the Consignment of the Keys to St. Peter and the Conversion of St. Paul, attached to the walls above the choir, painted by Giovan Battista Lombardelli della Maria in 1591.

The choir is certainly one of the most beautiful to be found in Italy. It was begun in 1525-26 by Bernardino di Luca Antonibi of Perugia with the collaboration of Niccolò di Stefano of Bologna. After a long interruption, probably owing to the plague, the work was resumed in 1533 by Stefano di Antoniolo Zambelli of Bergamo and his assistants (Grisello, Tommaso, Nicola and Antonio from Florence; the Bolognese artist, Battista; the French-man, Ambrogio; the Dalmatian, Domenico Schiavone and Niccolò di Antonio di Ludovico from Cagli). The work was finished in 1535. The signature of Stefano da Bergano is visible at the head of the cymatium. The beautiful door of the choir depicts the Annunciation and Moses saved from the Red Sea and was made by Frà Damiano of Bergamo brother of Stefano, in 1536 (his signature and the date are visible beneath the railing). The large lectern in the choir was made in 1536-37 by two of Stefano's assistants: Battista from Bologna and Ambrogio from France. From the inlaid door, we pass onto a small terrace affording a splendid view of the Assisi valley.

of a certain Maestro Dionigi (1615).

The main altar was originally decorated with paintings by Giannicola di Paolo and with Perugino's famous Ascention, now in the Museum of Lyon; it was completely remade by Valentino Martelli between 1592 and 1608. Martelli also designed the ciborium, made in Rome by Ghetti between 1627 and 1635. The large canopy above the altar is the work of Benedetto Bandiera who also painted the Four Evangelists on the vault (1591) and the canvas in the apse depicting the Death of St. Benedict.

Wooden choir and frescoes in the apse (16th century).

Entering the north aisle, on the far wall, there is a Pietà between SS. Jerome and Leonard, dated 1469 and thought to be an early work of Fiorenzo di Lorenzo (though some believe it to be the work of Benedetto Bonfigli or Nicolò del Prione). Below it, we

find the tombstone of Bishop Ugolino da Montevibiano (+ 1319). A painting depicting Christ in the Garden, attributed to Giovanni Lanfranco (17th century) hangs in the left-hand corner. There follows the entrance of the Vibi Chapel, built in 1473 and renovated in 1506 by Francesco di Guido of Settignano. The work was financed by Baglione Vibi, a nobleman from Montevibio. The splendid marble altar-frontal showing the Child Jesus, the Baptist and St. Jerome is agreed to be the work of Mino da Fiesole (1473, see inscription). Within the lunette above this, there is an Annunciation by Giovan Battista Caporali (1521) who is also author of the remaining decorative fragments on the walls and vault. To the left is a painting of the Visitation by Polidoro di Stefano Ciburri of Perugia (1530); to the right, we see a copy of Giovanni Spagna's Ma-

donna of the Lily by Sassoferrato.

Returning into the aisle, we find ourselves directly in front of a painting of St. Paul the Apostle after the style of Guercino; a little further ahead, on the opposite wall, there is a painting of Christ laid in the Tomb, copied from Baglioni di Raffaello's Deposition by Sassoferrato (the original is in the Borghese Gallery in Rome). The next chapel, which first belonged to the Baglioni family and then to the Ranieri family, was also built to a plan by Francesco di Guido of Settignano (1505). The vault, origi-

1. Mino da Fiesole(?): gold-plated marble altar-frontal (15th century). 2. Fiorenzo di Lorenzo(?): Pietà (15th century) and details of St. Geronimo and St. Leonard. 3. Wooden choir: detail (16th century). 4. Giovan Battista Salvi (Sassoferrato): Judith with the head of Holophernes (17th century).

nally decorated with frescoes by Giovan Battista Caporali, now bears paintings by Annibale Brugnoli (1863); on the left-hand wall, we see a painting of Jesus in the Garden by Guido Reni; on the right, there is a canvas depicting Jesus with Veronica by the Bolognese artist, Giovan Francesco Gessi (17th century). Opposite the chapel there is a painting of St.

4

Paul. On the walls in front of this, we find a canvas by Sassoferrato (17th century) depicting Judith with the head of Holofernes.

Next is the Chapel of the Sacrament with a vault decorated by Francesco Appiani with perspective square panels by Pietro Carattoli (1762-63); above the altar hangs an ancient image of the Madonna of the Lily of the Perugian school; this work dates back to the early 1500's and was taken from the Valiano villa in 1643; on either side, there are paintings (SS. Peter and Paul) by Giovan Battista Wicar (19th century). The right-hand wall bears a large canvas by Giorgio Vasari (1566) showing the Prophet Elijah and St. Benedict. The left-hand wall has a painting of St. Benedict sending St. Marius to France by Giovanni Fiammingo (16th century) and the Wedding of Cana by Vasari.

Back in the aisle, on the following column, there is an Adoration of the Magi by Eusebio da San Giorgio (1508). A staircase leads down into excavations recently carried out which reveal the foundations of a pre-existing structure dating back to the High Mediaeval period.

The next altar we come to has an Assumption of Our Lady by Orazio Alfani (16th century). Further on, we come to an Annunciation by Sassoferrato and an altar with a wooden Cru-

cifix, dating 1478 and attributed the Eusebio Bastoni of Perugia. A little further ahead, the panel showing the Pietà is a late work by Perugino and originates from the Church of St. Augustine. The next altar has a painting of St. Peter Vincioli by Appiani (1751). At the end of aisle, the paintings of St. Marius and St. Placido are by Giacinto Giminiani (1677).

Next to the canvases by Giminiani, we find a door leading into a room containing many precious illustrated books (hymnals, catechisms, graduals and antiphonaries) originating from the 15th and 16th centuries.

Returning into the first cloister through a corridor on the left, which reveals the impressive foundations of the bell-tower, we enter the second, Renaissance-style, main cloister attributed to Francesco di Guido of Settignano (16th century); it has a well in the centre by Galeotto di Paolo of Assisi (1530). Under the portico on the west side, we can still see the door and two mullioned windows of the former Charter House. Further on, we come to the entrance of the ancient refectory, the atrium of which contains a fine lavabo with a large stained-glass lunette showing the Woman of Samaria at the well; it is attributed to the Florentine artist, Benedetto de Zuanni, alias 'Buglione' (1487-88). Passing through another corridor, we

leave the main cloister and enter the 'new' cloister (also called the Cloister of the Stars) which was designed by Alessi in 1571.

Today, the monastery is the seat of the Foundation of Agricultural Education, formed in 1887, and the Faculty of Agriculture of the University of Perugia.

In front of the Abbey is the fine **Frontone Garden**; Braccio Fortebracci, governor of Perugia from 1416 to 1424, used this space as a weapon store; from 1569 on, it became the location of the livestock market which took place during the All Saints' Day Fair. At the beginning of the 1700's, the site was donated to the Arcadians; this marked the beginning of its transformation into a pleasant garden; between 1778-80, the amphitheatre was built, at the centre of which is an arch designed by Baldassare Orsini, erected in 1791.

One leaves the monastery grounds via **porta di St. Costanzo** which was designed by Valentino Martelli and built in 1586-87. It comprises laterie columns above which is the coat-of-arms fo the Abbey of St. Peter. This is surmounted by a large cornice and an attic which contains the coat-of-arms of Sextus V in travertine stone. (The mediaeval porta of St. Costanzo is situated in the Botanical Gardens of the Faculty of Agriculture).

1. The Main Cloister. 2. Palazzo della Penna.

La Rocca Paolina

From Via Podiani, we enter Viale Indipendenza. A short way ahead, turning immediately to the right into Via Marzia, we can walk alongside the last remaing spur buttress of the **Rocca Paolina**.

It is documented that the Rocca Paoliona was a concrete political and military symbol of authority over the «riotous city». In fact, this fortress was built by Paolo III after the salt war in order to keep the city under control once and for all. It was built to a design by Antonio and Aristotile da Sangallo in record time (1530-1543). A quarter of the city was demolished in order to construct it (the houses of the Baglioni family, the St. Giuliana

quarter, the Church of St. Mary of the Servants and many others). Sangallo managed to save the Etruscan **Porta Marzia** by integrating in into the wall structure, leaving it still visible above the doorway. The porta is a composed of an arch underlined by a row of hewn rocks and a slightly protruding cornice. A horizontal strip, bearing the inscription *Augusta Perusia* acts as a base to a gallery comprising Italo-Conrinthian pillars between which five figures are placed. This ensemble is symmetrically arranged between two Italo-Corinthian columns, parting from the base of the arch which, together with the other smaller columns, support the upper protruding cornice bearing the inscription *Colonia Vibia*. The Three figures in the gallery have been identified as Gastor, Jove and Polluce. On the sides, there are two figures of horses. The jambs of the door are visible, in their original position, at the entrance of the Rocca. Inside, we recognise traces of ancient roads (Via Bagliona etc.), piazzas, buildings and towers which were incorporated into the foundations of the fortress. It was an impressive edifice based around a wast central nucleus, linked by a long corridor (120 metres approximately) to the sentry areas towards the city's edge. Within this central complex, there stood the Captain's Palace, designed by Galeazzo Alessi, and adorned by a beautiful loggia, also designed by Alessi (although some believe it to be the work of Raffaello da Montelupo); the rooms of the building had frescoes by various artists: Cristoforo Gherardi, alias the 'Doceno' of Borgo St. Sepolcro, Vasani Lattanzio della Marca, Raffaellino del

1. The Rocca Paolina (interior): movable stairs. 2. The Rocca Paolina and Porta Marzia. 3. A. Iraci: Pictorial reconstruction of the Rocca Paolina.

Colle, Dono Doni, Tommaso da Papacello. The sculpture work was done by Simone Mosca da Settignano. Today, all that remains is the south-west buttress; the fortress, symbol of the papal yoke, was destroyed immediately after the Unification.

Proceeding along Via Marzia, on the left, we see the Lomellina Fountain, built by order of Lorenzo Lomellini, Governor of the city from 1678 and 1685.

At the end of Via Marzia, we come to Via Baglioni, on the right, and **Piazza Italia**, on the left.

Whilst the Piazza Grande represented the political, civil and religious focal point of the city during the communal epoch, another piazza was destined to assume a different symbolic value during the second half of the 19th century.

After the destruction of the Rocca Paolina, by 1862, the city began to think about the reconstruction of the area in which the fortress has been located. Piazza Italia, or Piazza Vittorio Emanuele as it was then called, came to characterise this area during the late 1800's. At the end of the 70's, the building designed by Alessandro Arienti was completed and became the seat of the provincial administration and the prefecture. This building stands at the centre of the square. It contains frescoes by D. Bruschi. In 1871, the building of the Banca Nazionale (today, the Banca dItalia) was erected, based on a design by G. Rossi. Between 1870-72, a large building was constructed to the left, designed by the Perugian architect, Guglielmo Calderini, for use as private apartments. In 1880, the wealthy Perugian, Sig. Brufani, obtained the area bordering the Banca Nazionale in order to build a hotel of the same name. In 1897, the Communal Council accepted the proposal to assign a large area of the piazza beside Palazzo Donini to Sig. Cesaroni, another wealthy Perugian who had become rich through commercial speculation. Cesaroni built himself a luxurious private house, a symbol of the city's new middle-class wealth. This villa was designed by Guglielmo Calderini and contains Art Nouveau frescoes by A. Brugnoli. Today, this palazzo belongs to the Regional Government. The following words have been used to describe this illustrious piazza — «The buildings surrounding the new piazza constitute a typical expression of bourgeois culture and taste and provide for all the needs and tendancies of the unitary state: the Government building, the headquarters of the Banca Nazionale, the luxury hotel, the large apartment block and the plush residence of the rich middle-class man».

The pre-existing **Palazzo Donini** stands out against this background. It is Perugia's most beautiful 18th-century palazzo and wass erected between 1716 and 1724. It is situated on the corner of Corso Vannucci and Piazza Italia and presents a double array of cornices and a triple array of windows with curved and coned pediments, all in travertine. The two doors facing the Corso and Piazza are adorned by two columns with travertine cushions supporting a balaustrade. The interior, with its rich store of 18th-century decorations, represents the most conclusive proof of Perugian artistic culture during the period in question. The elegant lay-out, with the suggestive perspective arrangements by Pietro Carattoli and the refined formal touches of Francesco Appiani (and also Anton Maria Garbi, Francesco Brizi and Giacinto Boccanera), give an excellent demonstration of the sumptuous decorative tastes of the aristocratic nobility of the time.

In Corso Vannucci, beside Palazzo Donini, is the small **Church of St. Mary of Ranson**, built in 1578, restored in 1657, and at one time decorated by Francesco Appiani.

Behind the Prefecture building are the Carducci Gardens, affording a splendid and vast panorama: from the mountains of Nocera and Gualdo to Subasio, the Foligno and Clitunno vallies and as far as the mountains to the west which mask Lake Trasimeno.

From Piazza Italia, continuing along Corso Vannucci, we return into Piazza Grande. Taking Via Baglioni, we go back to Piazza Matteotti.

Immediately on the right, at the beginning of Via Baglioni, we find the ancient parish **Church of St. Lucy**, documented as early as 1285; deprived of its parishioners after the construction of the Rocca Paolina, it was conceded by Cardinal Fulvius Della Corgna, Bishop of Perugia, to the college of the City Clergy. It took on its present physiognomy between 1760 and 1770. The relief work in the vault is by Valentino Carattoli, the scenes from the life of St. Lucy are by Francesco Appiani and Carlo Spiridione Mariotti; above the altar is a canvas by Giulio Cesare Angeli, representing the Virgin and Child in glory with St. Ivo and St. Lucy at their feet (17 century).

At the end of Via Baglioni, near Piazza Matteotti (no. 3), we find the aristocratic Palazzo Alfani-Florenza, the entrance of which is the work of Vignola.

A thoroughfare of the Rocca Paolina.

5 Itinerary

The Church of S. Spirito -
The Church of St. Prosperus -
The Church of St. Juliana.

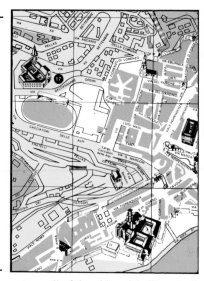

The course of Corso Vannucci is interrupted by the opening into Piazza della Repubblica which is dominated by the 17th-century Palazzo Baldeschi (no. 66); the former parish church of St. Isidor, included in the Cathedral Charter as early as 1163, and the present day façade of which is attributed to Giulio Danti; and the **Teatro del Pavone** which was built by a group of nobles between 1717 to 1723 and reconstructed to a design by Pietro Carattoli during the second half of the 18th century.

On the left side of the piazza, we find Via Baldo: at no. 10, a plaque records the fact that the famous Judge, Baldo degli Ubaldi lived here (1320/27-1400); he is the most famous Perugian alongside Bartolo da Sassoferrato of whom he was a pupil.

On the right side of the Piazza, we turn into Via Bonazzi. To get an idea of the «secret parts» of Perugia, devoid of famous monuments, but none the less interesting owing to its narrow street, hidden corners, mediaeval buildings (warehouses, tower/houses etc.), we can wander along Via delle Streghe, turning into Via della Sapienza and returning to Via Bonazzi by Via del Bufalo, at nos. 10 and 14 of which, we can see clear evidence of square-shaped towers. At no. 10 in Via Bonazzi, we come across the remains of the outer wall of the old parish **Church of St. Biagio**. Part of the contents of the church are to be found in the modern church of SS. Biagio and Savino in Via G. Bigazzini. It contains the altar-piece by Anton Maria Fabrizi (the altar on the left) depicting the Madonna and Child, St. Octavian and St. Appollonia (1644) and the altar-piece by Vincenzo Angeli (right) showing one of St. Biagio's miracles (1797).

Between nos. 37 and 39 of Via Bonazzi, there is the **Church of Suffrage**. The Order of Our Lady of Suffrage, whose cause was to pray for the souls in Purgatory, was established in the Church of St. Mary of the Hill (porta St. Pietro) in 1619; in 1639, it found its permanent home here. Inside, above the main altar, we find the Birth of the Virgin by the Perugian artist, Giovanni Francesco Bassotti (17th century). It also preserves a wooden crucifix by Giampietro Zuccari which was completed by Leonardo Scaglia during the 17th century.

Next door to the Church is **the Oratory of SS. Crispin and Crispinaino** which belonged to the Guild of Shoemakers. This guild was founded in

The Mandorla Gate.

1613 and started building its present seat in 1618 (the church was consecrated in 1625). Above the main altar is a small travertine coat-of-arms showing the shoemakers' knife. To the left, is the massive Palazzo Ansidei, possessing an Alessian loggia overlooking Via Mario Grecchi.

Turning right, we enter Via Caporali. At nos. 3 and 10, we can see a tower/house among the other buildings.

Taking Via del Pozzo, at no. 8, there is a mid-16th century courtyard with a stone recording the fact that Galileo Galilei was once a guest here. We exit into Viale Indipendenza: immediately on the right we can see the Donati Tower (restored) and, at the far end, the Etruscan wall and porta della Mandorla. Past this, further along Viale Indipendenza, we come across Via Fatebenefratelli, on the left, and Via del Circo, on the right. Turning into Via Fatebenefratelli, we arrive at the hospice, **church and monastery**, built by the religious communuty of the **Order of St. Giovanni di Dio**, established here during the late 16th and early 17th centuries. The main altar of the church has a canvas depicting the Virgin, St. John and St. John Evangelist, patron saint of the Order; it is a work by Francesco Laudati (18th century). The Sacristy contains the lunette which used to be placed over the main door; there are also frescoes representing the Virgin, SS. Nicholas and St. John (late 16th early 17th centuries).

Via del Circo takes its name from the presence of a building housing a juggling circus, constructed between 1804 and 1808, and demolished after 1860. At the beginning of Via Torcoletti, is the **Church of St. Savino**, now a carpentry work-shop. The parochial title of St. Savino was transferred here following the construction of the Rocca Paolina; the original church — listed in the Cathedral Charter as early as 1036 — was demolished.

Continuing along Via Caporali, we find ourselves infront of the **Parish Church of St. Angelo at porta Eburnea**. This church probably already existed as early as the 11th century, three quarters dependent on the Abbey of Pomposa and one quarter on the Cathedral Charter; in 1285, it was listed among the parish churches. It took on its present form in the early 1800's when it was redesigned by Antonio Stefanucci; its façade is neoclassical in style. Above the main altar, there is a canvas depicting St. Michael between St. Francis Salesio and St. Ursula by Cristoforo Gasperi (1750 circa); left of the altar, is another canvas by Gasperi representing the Virgin and Child with SS. Lucy and Apollonia (1745); to the right, is a painting by Domenico Garbi depicting St. Michael casting Satan out of Paradise with a host of angels supporting an oval cornice in which can be seen Our Lady of Humility (1800).

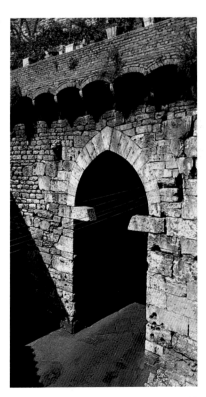

The Church of S. Spirito (the Holy Spirit)

Beyond the porta, on the left, we turn into Via del Parione; after a short stretch of road, we find ourselves in front of the **Church of S. Spirito**. This was the seat of a Benedectine female community, listed among the Perugian dependencies of the Abbey of Farneta, in a document drawn up by Henry II in 1014, although several doubts exist as the validity of this document. However, the convent certainly existed in the 13th century. In the early 15th century, after a series of mergers had taken place, the convent ceased to exist. The site was given to the Minimi family in 1576, and the construction of a new church commenced in 1578 following a design by Giovanni Francesco Vezzosi of Pistoia. It was completed in 1689 and consacrated in 1691. At present, it functions as a parish church. The classical interior has a wall divided into three separate sections, each of which has an arch acting as a niche for an altar; the curved gallery is scanned by five blind arches.

The first two altars, right and left of the nave, contain false architectural perspective by Pietro Carattoli (18th century). The first altar on the right is host to a Madonna and Child with St. Michael the Archangel by Francesco Busti (18th century). The following altar shows the Trinity contemplated by SS. Gaspar of Valenza, Leonardo de' Longobardis and Francis Salesio, by Cristoforo Gasperi (1788). The third altar, in carved gold-plated wood dating back to the late 1600's, has a central niche contining an image of St. Francis of Paolo (17th century). The large canvas at the centre of the apse, depicting the Descent of the Holy Spirit, is the work of Lazzaro Baldi. The canvas on the right shows St. Peter giving Baptisms and the one on the right shows St. Peter giving Confirmations; both works originate from the Baldi school (17th century). The pews,

1. The Church of the Holy Spirit: Interior (17th century). 2. The Church of St. Prosperus: High Mediaaeval Ciborium (7th - 8th century).

made out of walnut in the Choir, date from the 18th century. The inner-façade wall bears two canvases attributed to Mattia Batini (18th century). From here, the left-hand wall of the nave has an altar which is host to a canvas by Giacinto Boccanera (1731) depicting St. Spiridione administering the Sacrament of Baptism to Emperor

Costante. The second altar (the altar of the goldsmiths) has a canvas by Mattia Battini (18th century) depicting Andronicus and Atanasia expressing resignation for the loss of their children. The third altar comprises a relief in carved multicoloured wood with decorative stucco-work (18th century).

Returning along Via del Parione, wer turn into Via S. Giacomo. At no. 50, we notice the travertine Renaissance portal of the former **Parish Church of St. Giacomo** of porta Eburnea (1285 circa), now used as a warehouse. Going ahead, we take Via delle Forse at the end of which we come across the mediaeval porta S. Giacomo (of St. James); if, on the other hand, we prefer to go down Via Eburnia, we come to the 16th-century **porta Eburnea** (1576) built by order of Governor Santacroce (for this reason, sometimes referred to as porta Crucia), and attributed to Valentino Martelli. Here, as elsewhere, we recognise a case of a mediaeval borgo which developed outside the city walls creating the necessity of new walls and new city gates; thus, both the ancient porta Eburnea and the mediaeval porta of St. Giacomo are clearly visible.

The Church of St. Prosperus

Coming out of Via Eburnea and turning right, we cover a short stretch o Viale Pompeo Pellini and then turn left into Via S. Prospero in order to visit the church of the same name.

It is commonly thought that the foundations of the **Church of St. Prosperus** dated back to the 7th or 8th centuries; it was certainly a religious and cultural centre during the early 13th century when Bonamico worked there; in 1285, it was listed among the parish churches of the porta Eburnea area; in 1302, we find it in the Cathedral Charter to which it belonged until the end of the 16th century although, in 1436, it was included among the properties of the Abbey of Pomposa. In 1609, it became a seminary; during the 18th century it was

taken over by the Missionary Fathers and finally by the Donini family; after this, the church traversed a period of neglect and decline up to around 1920, then it was re-opened by the original order when important frescoes were discovered by Ettore Ricci (1927).

The Church of St. Juliana
(S. Giuliana)

Returning from St. Prosperus, we take Viale Pellini, Via Fiorenzo di Lorenzo and then turn right into Viale Baldassarre Orsini. A short distance ahead, we reach the **Church and former Convent of St. Juliana**.

Although precise information regarding its pre-history is lacking, the official date of the foundation of the convent was 1253, when a group of papal letters and a solemn favour were sent to the Perugian convent by Pope Innocent IV, declaring it to be under the protection of the Holy See, affirming the rules of the Benedictine Order according to the Cistercian statue, conceding it ecclesiastical privileges and confirming its ownership of its acquired properties. It was the Cistercian Cardinal, Giovanni da Toledo, who promoted the consolidation of this new and powerful female monastic movement when in the same year (1253), he assigned the convent to the jurisdiction of the Abbot of St. Galgano (Diocese of Volterra), an act which was confirmed by the Abbot of Citeaux in 1260. The origins of the Cistercian convent are to be found outside the city, though nearby, between porta S. Pietro and Porta Eburnea. It is almost as if its development was intended to counterbalance that of the Poor Clares at Monteluce (cf. further on). Thanks to the support of the city's most important families, the convent became one of the richest and most prestigious in Perugia. From the 14th century on, the convent entered a phase of moral decline and decadence which culminated in the early-16th century, by which

The Church and Garden of St. Juliana.

time the nuns completely ignored the rules of community life within the cloister. The ill fame of the monastery, which probably provided the background for Agnolo Firenzuola's most riqué short story, reached the ears of the popes and Paul III attempted a reform of the convent. In 1567, Pius V placed it under the direct jurisdicion of the Bishop of Perugia, definitively severing it from the Cistercians. All subsequent bishops were diligent in the reform of the convent throughout the late-16th century; its religious and moral welfare appears to have improved during the 17th century. With the Napoleone suppression, the

Church was used as a granary; after the Unification, it became (and still is) a military hospital. The church was reopened in 1937.

The double skewed façade, covered in red stone squares bordered by strips of white, has a portal with a rounded arch decorated with a trilobe and capitals bearing finely carved acanthus leaves. There is an identical doorway on the north flank of the Church. Above is an elegant rosewindow.

Its aisleless, tie-beamed interior reveals numerous traces of its ancient pictorical decoration. From the surviving fragments we deduce that the far wall was host to a large composition. On the walls of the nave, traces are still visible of an upper decorative strip more or less at the level of the windows. Another strip, about four metres in width, began at ground level and ran along all the walls of the building. The triumphal arch, major sections of which still remain, was decorated both externally and internally. The exterior surface of the piers still bears 'larger than life' figures: on the right, St. Juliana; on the left, St. Bernard of Chiaravalle holding the crosier and rules of the order.

If we prefer not to descend via the Porta della Mandorla, we can take an alternative ruote, following Via Annibale Mariotti. At no. 2, there is a fine 15th-century cloister with secular frescoes. Further ahead, we find ourselves in Piazza Mariotti. The convento of the Poor Nuns (or of Monna Simona) stood in this square, governed by the rule of the Servants of Mary; this community grew up during the 15th century and expanded after the suppression of the parish church of St. Batholomew (1615), during the early 17th century. Today, the area occupied by the convent is used for private apartments and secular activities. Overlooking the piazza, is the **Church of the Brotherhood of the 'Annunziata'** (first documented in 1334) which had its seat between the convent of the Poor Nuns and the Parish Church of St. Bartholomew; after the suppression of the latter, the convent took over the monks previous establishment, whilst the Brotherhood occupied the former parish church. Today, it contains frescoes by Domenico Bruschi (1900-1901).

Passing under an archway, we ar-

Capital of the Cloister (13th century).

rive in Via della Cupa. From here, we can admire one of the best preserved stretches of the ancient Etruscan city wall. The Commune was always very diligent its protection and renovation of this area of Perugia. Evidence of mediaeval restoration in clearly visible in the presence of younger travertine, calcareous rock and sandstone. On the left flank we see the results of the numerous attempts at reinforcement of the more precipitous sections.

At no. 5, we find the **College della Sapienza Vecchia** (now used as a boarding school for orphans). It was founded by Cardinal Nicolò Capocci in 1361 to accomodate young men who had been reccomended by bishops from all over Europe, so that they could study at the Perugian *Studium* free of charge. The building was completed in 1369. The travertine portal we see today is in the Renaissance style. The main courtyard contains a cistern surmounted by a twelve-sided well curb with small columns at each corner. This is thought to have been built at the same time as the college but the six columns supporting the architrave and hexagonal cornice were added at the end of the 16th century. The chapel contains a fragmented late-16th century Crucifixion.

Next door to the College della Sapienza, is the ancient **Church of St. Mary of the Valley**, listed among the dependencies of the Abbey of Farneta in an uncertain document supposedly issued by Henry II in 1014. If this document is false, it is still certain that the church depended on Farneto, as affirmed in a favour issues by Pope Adrian IV in 1155 and by Clement III in 1188. It was the ancient seat of hermit monks and perhaps of the Carmelite brothers. From 1285 to 1733, it was a parish church. In 1760, it passed into the hands of the Builders' Guild — named after St. Marino — founded in 1578 and having has several different seats prior to this; the church was restored in 1771. Towards the end of the 19th century the guild dispersed. Today, the church and its annexes belong to the Oblate Sisters of St. Francis of Sale. The interior of the church is neoclassical in style and contains a large canvas depicting the Assumption of the Virgin between SS. Lawrence and Charles Borromeo by Simeone Ciburri (1612 circa). There is also an 18th-century painting of St. Francis of Sales, a Pietà dating back to the 17th century and an 18th century painting of St. Marino. Taking Via della Luna and turning left, we see the apse of the mediaeval church.

Continuing along Via della Cupa, we turn left to find the entrance to the Cupa Gardens which follow the course of the Etruscan wall. A short distance ahead, we come to Piazza del Drago; passing beneath an archway, we arrive in a small square from which we can see the walls of the Cupa; to the right, we see the imposing edifice — with protrunding apse — of St. Benedict's. Its exact historical background is unknown except for the fact that it belonged to the Knights of Malta at least from the end of the 13th century. During the late-18th century, the Benincasa Conservatory was founded in this area, enlarged between 1777 and 1784, to accomodate and instruct young girls from the age of twelve until finding them a definitive employment.

From Piazza del Drago we take Via Benincasa and turn into Via Deliziosa where, at no. 10, we find the mediaeval double-skewed façade and belltower of the former parish **Church of St. Antony**, listed among the dependencies of the Cathedral Charter as early as 1163; this parish merged with that of the **Church of Santa Croce** — situated further along Via Benincasa — in 1802; at no. 17, we find a plaque recording the fact that the famous artist, Perugino, lived here.

At the end of Via Deliziosa, we go back into Via della Cupa; turning left, we return into Via dei Priori.

6 Itinerary

The Church of the Company of Death - The 'New' Church of St. Mary - The Church of St. Antony Abbot - The Church of St. Mary of Monteluce - The Church of St. Bevignate - The Church of St. Simone del Carmine - the Church of St. Fiorenzo.

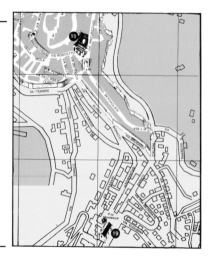

The Church of the Company of Death
(Compagnia della Morte)

Piazza Piccinino is bordered by the 17th-century Palazzo Sorbello. Inside, we find as Etruscan well and **Church of the Company of Death**. The Company was founded in 1570 with the aim of providing a decent burial for poor Christians found dead in the streets of the town; although devoid of its original meaning, the company still exists. The construction of the building was begun in 1575, both supervised as well as designed by Bino Sozi of Perugia; works went on until their completion at the beginning of the 1600. The church has the shape of a Greek Cross with a cupola placed above a high tiburio; the elegant Mannerist doorway was completed in 1606. The interior was renovated during the 18th century and has numerous stucco-work decorations and interesting paintings. Beginning from the right arm of the Cross, the first canvas on the right depicts St. Antony and the Virgin and Child — a work by Francesco Busti (18th century); the painting of St. Peter of Alcantara and the one depicting St. Francis Saverio are by the same author.

The 'New' Church of St. Mary

Descending a series of steps, we turn into Via del Roscetto, at the end of which, on the left, is situated the **New Church of St. Mary** (S. Maria Nuova). Without doubt, this was a parish church in 1285, although it had probably been one for quite some

2

time previous to this. It passed into the hands of the Sylvestrines between the end of the 13th century and the beginning of the 14th century; it remained with the monks until the construction of the Rocca Paolina which brought about the destruction of the Church of St. Mary of the Servants; at this point, S. Maria Nuova was taken over by the 'Serviti' (he Servants), whilst the Sylvestrine monks moved to the nearby Church of St. Fortunato.

The flank of the building is made up of a mediaeval wall with a portal and two ogival arches. The façade with its simple travertine doorway, is preceded by a double-flighted staircase and a fountain which was built in 1568 and restored in 1722.

The interior has a nave a two aisles and has vaulting which dates from the 16th century although it was restored during the 19th century. Traces of the old gothic structure are still visible in

1. The Gate of the Lilies (Porta dei Gigli).
2. The Church of the Company of Death: Vincenzo Pellegrini, All Saints (17th century).

the apse and in the chapels of the minor aisles. The innerfaçade wall is almost entirely occupied by the huge organ which was designed by Bino Sozi, carved by Marco Pace and decorated by Mattiuccio Salvucci (1612). To the right, in a low niche, there is a representation of the Immaculate Conception by Francesco Appiani of Perugia (18th century). The decorations in the nave, on the columns and intrados of the arches are the work of Bassotti, Amedei, Mazzi and Appiani. Originally, the lunettes above the cornice of the nave were also painted.

Beginning from the south aisle, the first altar, the Altar of the Crucifix, possesses a wealth of monumental architectural perspectives in multicoloured marble, attributed to Vincenzo Roscino (1600). On the left-hand side, a doorway leads into the Oratory of the Brotherhood of the Crucifix. This Brotherhood built its seat between the church and the con-

vent around the year, 1581.

The vault is decorated with false architectural perspectives by Pietro Carattoli; in the centre, we see the Glory of the Cross by Anton Maria Garbi (1750). The altar was designed by Valentino Martelli in 1593 and was once host to the Deposition from the Cross by Felice Pellegrini (1592-93), which is now situated above the door leading into the Sacristy.

Going back into the nave, the next altar is the Altar of the Banner. It contains the processional banner by Benedetto Bonfigli (1471) which depicts the Virgin Mary and SS. Benedict, Scolastic and Paolino Bigazzini imploring mercy for the people, whilst the angry figure of Jesus hurls thunderbolts onto the to-

1. The Church of St. Maria Nuova: the Alessian Bell tower (17th century). 2. Interior (16th century).

wered city of Perugia. The following altar is named after the Company of St. Juliana of the Lombards and originally contained an altar-piece by Andrea di Assisi which has since disappeared. The Chapel of Our Lady of Sorrows comes next. This was built in 1568 and restored in 1608. The 18th-century altar has now replaced the original one, which is thought to have the work of Martelli. It was once host to the Deposition by Stefano Amadei which is today situated in the south transept beside the Oltramontani altar. Amadei also painted the Presentation of Mary in the Temple and the Espousal, as well as the two small canvases on the intrados of the arch — Jesus Crowned with Thorns and St. Paul the Hermit. Corresponding to the original columns of the naves, we find a pulpit dating from the mid-1500's with a canopy painted with grotesques by Mattiuccio Salvucci. Entering the transept, the first

altar on the right is named after of Oltramontani Company, which moved here after leaving the Church of St. Mary of the Servants. Two niches on the side walls contain statues of St. Louis of France and St. Henry of Germany (17th century). The altar-piece depicting St. Helen worshipping the Cross is the work of Bernardino Gagliardi (18th century). There follows a door which leads into the Sacristy and Convent; above, we see the aforementioned painting by Felice Pellegrini, signed and dated by the artist (1593). The chapel at the far end contains traces of 15th-century frescoes and of the wooden arch of Braccio I Baglioni (+ 1479). Entering the gothic apse with its ribbed vault we admire the splendid wooden choir in the international gothic style, made in 1456, by Paolino di Giovanni of Ascoli and Giovanni da Montelparo, both from the Marches region of Italy. The chapel

on the left-hand side of the apse conserves fragmented frescoes depicting the Crucifixion and scenes from the life of St. Catherine by Lazzaro Vasani, great grandfather of Giorgio (15th century). Immediately next to this, there is a niche containing the figure of Christ between St. Bernardino and Stephen originating from the Umbrian school or the 15th century. At the head of the north transept, there is a 15th-century, carved and gold-plated altar. The altar-piece depicting the Virgin in Glory with SS. John the Baptist, Philip Neri and Philip Benizi is by Francesco Appiani (1740) and substitutes the fine Banner by Niccolò Alunno (1466), today situated in the Umbrian National Gallery. In the niche at the beginning of the aisle, there is a Virgin and Child between SS. Antony Abbot and Philip Benizi, signed by Scilla Piccinini (1585). The following altar (of the Madonna) is luxuriously carved and gold-plated (18th century) and is host to a Madonna and Child with SS. Peter and Paul, traditionally attributed to Iacopino del Conte but today thought to be the work of Girolamo Siciolante of Sermoneta (16th century). Above the side-door is an interesting painting of the Adoration of the Shepherds, probably the work of a Flemish artist (16th century). There follows the altar of the Seven Founders above which a copy has been placed of the Madonna between SS. Jerome and Francis by Perugino (1507), today housed in the National Gallery in London. The copy was painted by Giuseppe Carattoli during the 19th century. The next altar is named after St. Pellegrino and contains a canvas by Francesco Appiani depicting Jesus detaching himself from the Cross and going to meet St. Pellegrino and St. Juliana Falconieri. The small chapel at the far end is decorated with pleasant Mannerist-style stucco-work dating from the late 16th century and contains a

Madonna of Grace from the 15th-century Perugian school of painting.

Still at the end of Via del Roscetto, opposite S. Maria Nuova, we find the **Oratory of the Benedectine Brotherhood** which already existed as early as 1320. Its present form dates back to a 16th century reconstruction by Valentino Martelli (1598).

The interior still preserved the pictorial decorations of the vault (1610 circa) by Mattiuccio Salvucci (scenes from the lives of St. John the Baptist and St. Benedict) and on the lunettes (1665), by Giovan Francesco Bassotti and Giovan Battista Mazzi (scenes from the Old Testament).

From S. Maria Nuova, we may turn left into Via Pinturicchio. Inside no. 87, we find a 16th century cloister with laterite arches supported by travertine columns. This was part of che cloister of the now demolished Convent of the Servants. The belltower was begun in 1644 and built to a design by Galeazzo Alessi. At no. 62, we find the ancient **Monastery of St. Thomas** — first documented in 1274 — which originally belonged to

Wooden Choir (15th century).

the Cistercians but was passed into the hands of the Benedictine nuns from the mid-16th century on; in the period of suppression following the Unification it was converted to secular use. Of the monastery's church, there remains only the bell-tower in laterite stone. At no. 47, we can see Pinturicchio's house and at no. 1, a did of an Etruscan cinerary urs is visible. Via Pinturicchio leads into Piazza Fortebracci dominated by the Etruscan Arch and the Seat of the Foreign University.

The Church of St. Antony Abbot

Almost at the end of the street, on the right (nos. 101-102), is the **Church of St. Antony Abbot**, already a parish building are still evident in the façade and along the north flank. The church underwent its first transformation around 1450. Signs of the modificatons are visible in the fragments of Renaissance columns to be seen in the small cloister apposite the façade. A second renovation, sponsored by the Olive-

tans who took over the church in 1624-25, endowed the church with its present-day appearance. The loggia at the front of the building dates from the 18th century. The aisleless, barrel-vaulted interior conserves a beautiful organ in carved wood by Michele Buti of Pisa (1665); a canvas by Paolo Gismondi of Cortona (17th century) depicting St. Antony Abbot (now above the left altar, originally situated above che main altar); a 17th-century canvas by Benedetto Bandiera depicting the Child Mary and St. Anne (altar on the right); and four canvases portraying the Four Evangelists in the Presbytery area. The far wall bears frescoes by Gerardo Dottori (20th century). The Sacristy contains a rather damaged lunette painted in the 16th-century Perugian style as well as a canvas by Giovanni Andrea Carlone (1675 circa) depicting the Blessed Bernard Tolomei receiving the Habit and Rule from St. Benedict da Guido, Bishop of Arezzo.

Going back into Corso Bersaglieri, alongside the church, is a small piazza containing a drum of a Roman

column upon which is placed a stone pig (15th century), the symbol of St. Antony Abbot.

It is thought it also marked the point of access to the east wing of the Monmaggiore fortress which extended almost as far as the hill of Monteluce. This was the gate through which the Piedmont army of Manfredi Fanti entered Perugia in September 1859, in oder to liberate the city of Papal domination, defeating the Papal governor Schmid, who had been responsible for the Perugia Massacre on June 20th 1859).

The Church of St. Mary of Monteluce

Turning right after the porta, we find ourselves in Via Cialdini which runs alongside the laterite wall of the 16th-century reconstruction of the Rocca of Monmaggiore, attributed to Rocco di Vicenza (1519). At the end of this road, on the right, a small staircase takes us into Piazza di Monteluce where the remains are visible of three mediaeval shops in sandstone. An entire side of the Piazza is occupied by the **Church and former Convent of St. Mary of Monteluce**.

In 1281, Glotto Monaldi donated to Cardinal Ugolino, the future Gregory IX, a piece of land in the locality of Monteluce so that he could erect a church there as well as a convent and a residence for several women already living in the area. This was the official birth of the convent of St. Mary of Monteluce which was composed of a group of women following the example of St. Clare of Assisi and her companions. In the same year, Cardinal John of Perugia granted authorisation to build a church and convent. In 1219, Cardinal Ugolino ratified the convent, then in the process of being built; 1221 saw the papal confirmation of the convent by Pope Onorio III; in 1229, it was confirmed again by Gregorio IX (former Cardinal Ugolino). Proof that the convent was governed by the spiritual example of the Poor Clares, is provided, a *privilegian paupertatis* granted to the convent by Gregorio IX, also in 1229. The importance of the convent increased throughout the 13th century as is proved by the conspicuous number of letters and privileges issues by Popes Innocente IV, Alexander IV, Clement IV, Nicolò IV and Boniface VIII. During the 14th and 15th centuries, the convent traversed a period of moral and spiritual decadence from which it was eventually redeemed by drastic reforms backed by the firm support of the city's population and probably sponsored by St. John of Capestrano who stayed in Perugia during this period.

1. Tei Arch.
2. Anonymous artist of the 17th century: Angel figure.

During the course of the 16th, 17th and 18th centuries, the convent of St. Mary of Monteluce was one of the richest and most prestigious religious establishments in the area whilst maintaining a constant and high level of moral rigour. In 1703, the spiritual rule of the convent passed from the handsw of the Franciscan Observants into those of the Bishop, ie. the regular clergy of the diocese. Following the requisition of the convent in order to the convert it into a hospital (early 20th century), the sisters moved to the Church of St. Erminio (formerly St. Benedict's).

The façade which almost certainly belongs to the era of its renovation (1451), still preserves the mediaeval portal with a rounded arch rows of little columns in the plays. It is covered with the checkeres pattern composed of different coloured marble which is so typical of Perugian churches. Placed in correspondence to the bell-tower and in line with the façade wall, there is a small chapel.

The walls of the aisleless interior are entirely convered by a cycle of paintings executed probably between 1602 and 1607. They constitute an extremely interesting iconographical ensemble of Franciscan themes and subjects and it represents one of the best examples of Perugian Mannerism to be seen in the city. Although local sources tend to credit this work to Francesco Vanni and Giovanni Maria Bisconti, the poor condition of the frescoes prevent us from being able to advance a really convincing hypothesis at to the actual authors; this is even more difficult, when we bear in mind the greatly varied stylistic methods involved.

The presbytery, occupied in the centre by the main altar with pink marble and small gothic arches (13th century), contains a prospective decoration in stucco and gold-plated wood by Valentino Carattoni (18th century). The painting depicting the Coronation of the Virgin is a 19th-century copy of the original by Giulio Romano and Giovan Francesco Penni, today in the Vatican Art Gallery.

It was based on a drawing by Raphael and was painted in 1524-25. The predella, attributed to Berto di Giovanni, is today in the Umbrian National Gallery. On the right towards the base, there is a fine marble tabernacle by Francesco di Simone of Fiesole depicting the Eternal Father

Anonymous artist of the 17th century: St. Cosma.

114

among the church, the first chapel on the right has, on the intrados, the figures of the Eternal Father, the Four Evangelists and the Four Doctors of the Church.

At the far end of the church, a small door leads into the Sacristy, a large square-shaped ambient with a ribbed cross-vault. It was once the choir of the nuns. The shorter wall towards the church is decorated with 17th-century frescoes depicting the Flagellation and the Derision of Christ. A central niche contains a small carves wooden crucifix. Beneath this, we see images of saints and the Coronation of Our Lady (14th century). The long wall presents a series of 14th-century votive frescoes. From left to right they are: the Stigmata of St. Francis, St. Onofrio the Hermit, St. Michael the Archangel, the Baptism of Christ and four episodes from the life of St. Catherine (?) (the last two are much damaged). Traces of frescoes are also visible on the wall section immediately above this. Among the paintings hung on the walls, are the following: the Stigmata of St. Francis (17th century), a Glory of the Virgin and Saints (18th century) and a copy of Giulio Romano's Holy Family.

On leaving the church, we turn left into Via del Giochetto from which we can observe the side-wall of the same with its protruding buttresses, made in sandstone, in an architectural style similar to that of the Church of St. Bevignate and, outside Perugia, the Church of Montelabate. In the area opposite the church, the seasonal August Fair was held.

From Via del Giochetto we turn into Via del Favarone where, at no. 5, we find the **Convent of St. Paul of Favarone**. In 1264, this was private oratory for these who wished to pray for forgiveness. In 1317, it was presided over by a community of Sisters of Penitence which, in 1329, embraced the rule of St. Clare, thus constituting the Convent of Poor Clares which, in 1445, merged with the convent of St. Mary of Monteluce; this merger was

revoked in 1447 but confirmed in 1451. The Convent then became a place of retreat for the spiritual exercises promoted by the Jesuit father and by the Mission; after this, it became a holiday centre for seminary students. To this end, the building was renovated in 1790, to a design by Alessio Lorenzini. At present it is a private house. A trilobal gothic doorway is all that remains of the old building.

Going down Via E. Dal Pozzo, at no. 101, we see the Gate of the Lion which was designed by Galeazzo Alessi as an entrance to a suburban villa belonging to him.

The Church of St. Bevignate

Further ahead, is the **Church of St. Bevignate**. Who St. Bevignate actually was is no longer historically certifiable; local tradition has it that he was a hermit; it is certain that, from 1260 to 1300, frequent requests were made by the Commune's Council for the canonisation of this saint; this local cult was not officially recognised until 1605 by the Congregation of Rites. In 1243, the site was occupied by the Templar sect; work was begun on the building (at least as regards planning and design) in 1256; in 1283, the church was consacrated. It was built on or beside the site of a previous chapel named after St. Jerome. In 1312, following the suppression of the Templars, the church was taken over by the Knights of St. John of Jerusalem. Between 1324 and 1327, a female community adherring to the Order of St. John moved there; in 1517, the sisters left and the church returned into the hands of the Knights of St. John of Jerusalem, who let it 'in commenda'. It gradually became a simple. Abbey dependency of the Holy See. In 1860, it was secularised.

The double-skewed façade, bound by two robust buttresses, has a travertine round-archade doorway and a moulded rose-window. The north flank is similar in style to the architecture of St. Mary of Monteluce and St.

Mary of Valdiponte or Montelabate (near Parugia) and has a side door terminating in an ogival arch.

The aisleless interior is divided into two areas by ogival cross-vault. It may originally have had a tie-beamed ceiling similar to the one above the vault of St. Mary of Monteluce. The square-shaped apse also has a ribbed cross-vault and is illuminated by a large ogival mullioned window in travertine. Here, we find the oldest painting of the church, executed by local artists during the 1760's. Along the wall of the nave, the figures of the Apostles are arranged with large spaces between each. They are the work of a refined Byzantine-Style painter (late 13th century).

A rich decorative frieze runs the course of the entire wall of the church. It incorporates geometrical motifs, symbols and heraldic emblems and is thought to be the work of a local artist living during the late-13th century. The same artist was also author of the paintings in the two large lunettes located, one above the other, on the inner-façade wall. The first one, depicting scenes of battles between the Templars and Saracens, are of particular historical and religious interest.

Next door to the Church of St. Bevignate is a house with architectural forms similar to those of the Library of Monteripido.

The monumental **Cemetery of Perugia** is a short way ahead on the right. It was Gioacchino Pecci (the future Pope Leone XIII) who strongly promoted — after the government decree of 1836 — the construction of the cemetery, notwithstanding the strong opposition of the notibility and most of the tow's bourgeoisie. The Innauguartion took place on November 23rd 1849. The first

The Church of St. Bevignate.

project was designed by the communal engineer, Filippo Lardoni (1849), a second project for its extension was the work of Alessandro Arienti from Milan. The original cemetery already contained several monumental works of considerable architectural complexity, among which the following are of particular note: the sepulchral monuments of Prof. Lorenzo Massini by Raffaele Carattoli, son of Luigi; the tomb of the little Buattini child by Raffaele Carattoni and Raffaele Omicini; the tomb or the noblewoman, Francesca Perucchini by Giuseppe Luchetti; and of the Marquis Glotto Monaldi by Guglielmo Ciani, a pupil of Bartolini in Florence. After the enlangement of the cemetery, other impressive monuments were built, mainly by Francesco Biscarini and Raffaele Angeletti who, at the end of the century, opened a terracotta factory.

Further on, near the entrance of the new cemetery, is the **Church of St. Mary of Grace of Monterone**, designed in 1534 by Brother Giordano Tassi, in a sober and elegant style similar to that of the church of St. Mary of Light near porta St. Susanna. The façade, with travertine ashlarwork, is bordered on the sides by two pillars upon which rests a tympanum. There is a rose-window with elegant decorative motifs above the door.

On the return journey, we continue along Via Enrico Dal Pozzo which leads us through a zone knows as Fontenuova ad early as the 13th century; event today, a fountain, clearly incorporating mediaeval fragments, is still visible. It was in the locality of Fontenuovo that Raniero Fasani, father of the Discipline Movement attempted to establish his oratory Further ahead, where there now exists a marble workshop, was the site of the hospital church of the Shoemakers Guild, named after St. Crispino. It is possible that the hospital existed ad early as the 15th century; in 1737, it was combined with the large hospital of St. Mary of Mercy and, on this occasion the building was restored and enlarged. Today, we can admire its well-composed façade in white and red stone with a slender cornice composed of small medallions.

The Church of St. Simon of Carmine

At the end of Via Enrico Del Pozzo, we pass under an archway and enter Via dell'Asilo, once again among the tangle of narrow and characteristic city streets. After a brief stretch, we find the **Church of St. Simon of Carmine**, a parish church as early as 1285 and, without doubt, existing as early as 1233. According to Siepi, in 1296, it was donated to the Carmelites by the Bishop of Perugia.

The church's exterior bears numerous signs of the renovation works carried out at a various stages in its history: 1571, 1636, 1746 and 1852. Interesting traces of the mediaeval building are visible on the flank of the church (in Via Abruzzo). The aisless barrel vaulted interior — in its present form — belongs to the 19th-century renovation which completely transformed the decoration of the chapel and vaults, painted during the 16th and early-17th centuries by Simeone Ciburri, Cesare Sermei and Anton Maria Fabrizi. The ancient refectory (now part of the 'Santa Croce' nursery school in Via dell'Asilo no. 1) contains five lunettes depicting episodes from the story of the Prophet Elias by Anton Maria Fabrizi (17th century).

A short way beyond, we come to the **Oratory of the Brotherhood of SS. Simon and Fiorenzo** (Via Imbriani no. 41/b). The Brotherhood of St. Fiorenzo — near to the church and monastery of the name — already existed in 1337; that of St. Simon was officially established in 1371, already existed in the 1340's.

These tow brotherhoods merged sometime before 1571. The interior, the vault of which was originally decorated with frescoes by Pietro Carattoli (1724), has, above the altar, an interesting painting by Pietro Montanini (1674), depicting the Madonna and Child with SS. Simon, Fiorenzo, Francis and Antony.

Opposite the Church of St. Simon del Carmine, a flight of stairs takes us into the small piazza del Duca, which takes its name from the presence of an impressive palazzo belonging to the Dukes of Corgna (late-16th century).

Taking Via Imbriani, we can stop off in Via S. Giovanni del Fosso where, at no. 13, we see the former parish church of the same name, which was established in 1233. Over the centuries, the church was renovated several times. From Via S. Giovanni del Fosso, we enter into Via della Viola and, a short distance ahead, we find the begining of Via della Pazienza, where we can see the ancient Etruscan/Roman city wall in hewn travertine with evidence of a mediaeval restoration (1308) employing diverse materials (travertine, calcareous rock, sandstone and laterite).

If we walk to the end of Via Imbriani, before goingo up Via Alessi, we can turn into Via Bonaccia which leads us under the mediaeval Gate of St. Margaret; nearby, we can see traces of the mediaeval wall, even if this particular stretch has undergone drastic transformation. This was one of the steepest slopes of Perugia and, therefore, had need of frequent repair. The area opposite the gate — now occupied by the Psychiatric Hospital — was once the site of the Benedictine Convent of St. Margaret. It was supresed in 1810.

The Church of St. Fiorenzo

At the cross-road of Via Imbriani, Via Alessi and Via della Viola, we find the **Church and Former Monastery of St. Fiorenzo**.

This building, named after St. Fiorenzo the martyr, has very remote origins (8th century?). From the 11th century on, it belonged to the Abbey of St. Salvatore of Monte Acuto. When the abbey near Perugia was reformed, passing into the hands of the Cistercians, the monastery of St. Fiorenzo followed suit. During the 1440's, Eugene IV introduced there the Servants of Mary, thus eliminating all Cistercian influence and all forms of dependence on St. Salvatore of Monte Acuto.

The church was originally built in the gothic style; a few traces of this remain on the exterior: the foundations of the bell-tower, a small chapel with a single-arched window and several adjacent rooms. It was completely renovated during the second half of the 18th century to a design

by Pietro Carattoli (1768-70). The aisleless interior has — on the inner-façade wall — detached frescoes taken from the room next to the 16th-century cloister (others are preserved in a gothic hall parallel to the side wall of the church and in the parish office). Above the side-door, there is a 15th-century style painting by Giustino Cristofani (early-20th century). The first altar on the right by Francesco Appiani (18th century) depicts St. Pellegrino supported by an angel and Blessed John Porro. Backing onto the canvas, is a carved wooden Crucifix. The second altar which once belonged to the Ansidei family is host to a copy by Nicola Monti (18th century) of the famous altar-piece by Raphael (today in the National Gallery in London), which was located in the church up to 1764. The altar in the south arm of the transept has an interesting banner dated 1476, attributed to Benedetto Bonfigli, depicting an enraged Jesus with the beseaching figures of the Virgin and SS. Philip Benizi, Fiorenzo and Pellegrino Leziosi whilst an angel shows the penitent people a scroll on which is written a long reproof, the text of which is attributed to Spirito Gualtieri or Coppetta, both poets from Perugia. Below this, four episodes from the life of St. Philip Benizi are depicted. A niche in the centre of the presbytery contains a 14th-century fresco taken from the nearby Vicolo della Madonna in 1770 and restored in 1815 by Carlo Labrussi. The altar of the north transept, in stucco work by Benetto Silva (18th century), who also made the Banner altar, is host to a canvas by Francesco Silva (18th century) depicting the Virgin among the clouds and the seven Blessed Founders. The Sacristy contains interesting wardrobes dating back to the 17th century; it also has paintings on the lunettes depicting episodes from the life of St. Lawrence which are partly the work of Matteuccio Salvucci (1612) and partly (the right-hand wall) by Anton Maria Fabrizi (1630).

Returning along Via Alessi, we find ourselves back in Piazza Matteotti.

1. The Church of Carmine: a view of the left flank as seen from Via Abruzzo. 2. Cloister of the former Monastery of St. Fiorenzo.

I N D E X

Photographs:
Photographic Archives
Perugia Tourist Office
(photos Paoletti, Sacco, Tirilli)

Photographic Archives
of the Art History School of
the University of Perugia
(photos Giorgetti - Rome)

Foto Misano di A. Ascani
Foto A. Pesante - Perugia

Print:
Grafiche Zanini srl
Bologna (Italy)